THE
VEGETARIAN
POCKET BIBLE

THE
POCKET BIBLE
SERIES

THE
VEGETARIAN
POCKET BIBLE

CARYS MATTHEWS

WITH ANDREW SMITH

PB POCKET BIBLES

Important note

The information in this book is not intended as a substitute for medical advice. Neither the author nor the publisher can accept any responsibility for any injuries, damages or losses suffered as a result of following the information herein.

This edition first published in Great Britain 2012 by
Crimson Publishing, a division of Crimson Business Ltd
Westminster House
Kew Road
Richmond
Surrey
TW9 2ND

A catalogue record for this book is available from the British Library.

ISBN 978 1 907087 295

Typeset by IDSUK (DataConnection) Ltd
Printed and bound by CPI Clowes

ACKNOWLEDGEMENTS

A] massive] thank you to Jon (my vegetarian partner in crime) and] my] parents,] Delwyn and Jill (my greatest fans), for their unlimited]patience]and support, and for agreeing to sample my earlier vegetarian concoctions!

CONTENTS

INTRODUCTION

Whether you're new to vegetarianism or are a seasoned veggie, *The Vegetarian Pocket Bible* is packed full of guidance and useful tips on how to eat a nutritionally balanced *and* interesting vegetarian diet.

Although you'll find a wealth of information about all forms of vegetarian diets, this book focuses mainly on lacto-ovo vegetarianism. Chapter 1, 'Becoming Vegetarian', offers information on these different types and will help guide you through the first steps of managing your diet and embarking on a meat-free lifestyle.

The chances are you will be interested in the healthy credentials of the vegetarian diet and this book aims to help you get the most out of your meals. Chapter 2 will help you make sure that you're taking on the nutrients you need and also offers some specialist advice for older, diabetic or pregnant vegetarians. If you find yourself wondering where best to buy vegetarian alternatives, then Chapter 3 will help to fill you in. Suggestions about vegetarian shopping will include where to buy supplements and the best options for vegetarian delivery schemes.

Chapter 4 will look at cooking and the many ways in which you can spice up your veggie meals. The fifth chapter, 'Recipes', provides a tasty look into wholesome vegetarianism, offering a good range of vegetarian alternatives and easy to follow recipes.

Many veggies are real 'foodies' and have a passion for fine cuisine, and so the 'Eating Out' chapter offers advice on dining out and travelling as a vegetarian and suggests some great vegetarian places to try both in Britain and abroad.

The chapter on 'Children and Vegetarianism' focuses on young vegetarians and provides useful information explaining how children can safely follow a vegetarian diet. It also offers nutritious, vegetable-packed lunch ideas that children will love.

Finally, Chapter 8 offers a glimpse into the world of Veganism, explaining how it differs to vegetarianism and outlining some simple steps to becoming a vegan. Taking that next step and cutting out all animal products from your life can be challenging, but the advice in this chapter can help you succeed in adopting your new lifestyle. For vegetarians who fancy experimenting with vegan cooking there is also a handful of easy and tasty recipes you can rustle up in no time.

The most important consideration when living a vegetarian lifestyle is your own wellbeing. Remembering the environmental benefits and ethical merits of the lifestyle will help harden your resolve, though the diet is likely to be difficult if you are struggling. Keeping a relaxed and thoughtful attitude will help you to improve your lifestyle and hopefully this book can help put your mind at ease about quandaries and entertain you with interesting facts.

The world of vegetarianism is a vibrant and interesting one which tends to draw intelligent and engaged people towards it. Be sure to look to others around you for help and advice, whilst making sure that you put some real thought into your daily meals. Before you know it, you'll be feeling the profound benefits of a healthy, sustainable and exciting vegetarianism lifestyle.

Good luck and good health!

BECOMING VEGETARIAN

The decision to adopt a vegetarian diet can be an exciting and challenging prospect. Importantly, however, it will force you to really *think* about your food and this, in itself, should mean you begin to take new pleasure in your diet. Whatever your reasons for making the switch, this chapter will help alleviate any concerns you may have about 'going veggie'. By outlining the differing types of vegetarianism, you'll be able to ensure that you're fully aware of what the lifestyles entail. Likewise, looking at the different reasons for becoming a vegetarian will help you to know what is fuelling your desire to live a healthier, more ethical and often cheaper lifestyle. Changing your diet can be daunting, but the step-by-step approach outlined in this chapter, as well as the profiles of the different types of vegetarian diet you can choose to follow, can make the change easier and help your body become accustomed to a meat-free diet.

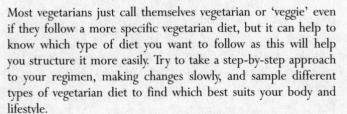 TYPES OF VEGETARIANISM

Most vegetarians just call themselves vegetarian or 'veggie' even if they follow a more specific vegetarian diet, but it can help to know which type of diet you want to follow as this will help you structure it more easily. Try to take a step-by-step approach to your regimen, making changes slowly, and sample different types of vegetarian diet to find which best suits your body and lifestyle.

Here are the various types of vegetarian diets you can consider, along with their respective pros and cons.

OVO-LACTO VEGETARIAN

Includes both dairy products and eggs.

This is the most common type of vegetarian diet in Western countries and this is the type of vegetarianism which will be the main focus of this book (aside from the later chapter on veganism).

Pros: This is the easiest vegetarian diet to follow as dairy and eggs can be eaten, which helps increase your choice of foods when cooking at home or eating out.

Cons: On the downside, this type of diet can encourage a reliance on dairy and eggs as replacement protein choices, rather than healthier options such as soya, tofu, lentils or pulses.

LACTO-VEGETARIAN

Includes dairy products but not eggs.

Pros: As with the lacto-ovo vegetarian diet, this is easy to follow and increases your options when cooking at home or eating out.

Cons: Many products contain egg so it will require a stricter approach to follow this type of vegetarian diet, as labels and ingredients will need to be checked carefully.

OVO-VEGETARIAN

No meat or dairy, but includes eggs.

Pros: Eggs provide an excellent source of protein and omega-3, so as an ovo-vegetarian you will benefit from having them in your diet. If you do eat eggs, your cooking options are slightly wider, although you need to be careful to check whether dairy is included.

Cons: You should avoid eating too many eggs as they contain higher levels of cholesterol than other foods. It is generally recommended by nutritionists to eat no more than two eggs a day, or just eat the egg whites which are healthier as they contain lower levels of cholesterol and are rich in protein.

VEGAN

Vegans choose to avoid consuming or using animal products. While other vegetarians choose not to eat meat (and potentially cut out eggs and milk, as above), vegans also avoid leather, fur, wool, and cosmetics or chemical products which have been tested on animals. Likewise, foods which are processed using animal products, such as refined white sugar or some wines, are unacceptable for vegans. Many vegans see their lifestyle as the natural extension of vegetarianism, designed to ensure that your life is free of any suggestion of cruelty or exploitation.

Pros: A vegan diet can be one of the healthiest, provided a sensible approach is taken to ensure nutritional needs are met. For further information, refer to Chapter 8, p.152, which provides more comprehensive advice on the vegan diet.

Cons: Eating a vegan diet can leave you prone to missing out on some vital nutrients, minerals and vitamins, as well as protein, if care is not taken to ensure your body's nutritional needs are met. Taking a good-quality vitamin supplement is recommended to avoid any deficiencies. For more advice on veganism, you may find it helpful to refer to the Vegan Society website, www.vegansociety.com.

Pocket tip 🌱

If you want to become a vegetarian, but don't want to give up dairy or eggs, try having a dairy-free Monday, or reduce the amount of dairy you eat by substituting it with protein alternatives such as pulses, nuts, soya and tofu.

(POLLO-)PESCATARIANS

Pollo-pescatarians (from the Latin words *pullus* meaning chicken and *pescis* meaning fish) eat both chicken and fish, but no red meat. Likewise, they may eat only fish, but no chicken or vice versa. This is not really a form of vegetarianism, though it can have health benefits for those seeking to move away from eating meat.

Pros: For those who want to continue to eat fish this is a popular choice and allows greater flexibility in cooking options and when eating out. Fish is also high in minerals and omega-3 fatty acids so there are some health benefits in eating oily fish occasionally.

Cons: In the UK over 14 million laying hens are currently housed in battery farms, but there has been a growing public interest in free-range farming practices. To help reduce battery farming practices, look for the words free-range, organic or RSPCA Freedom Food on the label. Other labels don't necessarily mean the chickens haven't been reared in intensive conditions.

Pocket fact 🌶

Almost a quarter of the world's population eats a mainly vegetarian diet. In 2009 3% of the UK adult population was vegetarian — a 1% increase on 2008.

🥕 WHY BECOME VEGETARIAN? 🥕

Vegetarianism can be a fantastic way to give yourself more energy, lose excess weight and follow an ethical lifestyle, as well as offering a range of other great reasons. The decision to become a vegetarian is likely to be personal and one that you feel passionately about because becoming a vegetarian is more complex than simply cutting meat and fish out of your diet. It is a lifestyle choice that is likely to affect how you view not only your food but potentially your ethical and political views.

There are many reasons people decide to adopt a vegetarian diet, and here we'll look at the main ones to help you weigh up the benefits of becoming a vegetarian.

HEALTH OR DIETARY REASONS

Many choose to adopt a vegetarian diet in the interests of their health. Thanks to the plethora of scientific studies that have been published in newspapers, magazines, journals, books, and websites, the general public are often more aware of the possibilities which a vegetarian lifestyle presents.

Prevention is the best cure

Vegetarians often make more informed choices about their food as a result of thinking more about its ingredients. By considering your diet more carefully, you can take steps towards preventing many of the illnesses associated with unhealthy lifestyles. The British Medical Association (BMA) produced one of the first reports advocating the health benefits of a vegetarian diet in 1986, titled *Diet, Health and Nutrition*. The report stated that if meat-eaters were to adopt a vegetarian diet their cholesterol levels, rates of obesity, heart disease, high blood pressure, cancer and bowel disease could all be significantly lowered. It also said that people can get all the minerals they need from a healthy and nutritious vegetarian diet.

The China Study, carried out by Dr T Colin Campbell over a period of 20 years, also analysed the links between health and nutrition. The initial findings, published in 1989, and later published as a book in 2005, highlighted the dietary differences between affluent Western countries and less affluent societies in the East. The study, which looked at the diet, lifestyle and health of 6,500 participants, revealed that the more affluent a society, the more meat was consumed and the higher the levels of cancer, heart diseases, strokes, high blood pressure and obesity. The study concluded that the largest single influence on the prevalence of these diseases was the amount of animal fat and protein eaten — the more these were eaten, the higher the risk of developing these conditions. The study ultimately concluded that a plant-based diet is more likely to promote good health and reduce the risk of such diseases.

This isn't to say that vegetarians are immune to these conditions, just that eating a healthy vegetarian diet helps reduce your chances of developing them.

Pocket fact

Evidence increasingly shows that people who consume a healthy vegetarian diet live longer. The world's oldest living person listed in the 2002 Guinness Book of Records was a Chinese woman, Du Pinhua, who was born on 22 April 1886 and reportedly lived to be 120 years old. Pinhua attributed her longevity to her lifelong vegetarian diet.

MAINTAINING A HEALTHY WEIGHT

Often people will adopt the vegetarian diet because they want to maintain a healthy weight. By eating a diet rich in fruit, vegetables, wholegrains, and pulses it is far easier to maintain a healthy weight, as a vegetarian diet tends to be lower in fat than a meat-eater's diet, which contains more saturated fat from meat or animal products.

A vegetarian diet can also help with weight loss, with vegetarians statistically being thinner than meat-eaters. A Cancer Research UK study looked at 22,000 people over a period of five years and found that those who cut out meat gained less excess weight than those who continued to eat meat. If you were someone who ate large portions of meat, then simply swapping this out for healthy vegetarian alternatives will likely see you lose weight immediately. Less saturated fat and a better standard of nutrition are two of the principle reasons for becoming a vegetarian.

Not all fats are bad!

Vegetarians tend to eat a diet higher in monounsaturated and polyunsaturated fats, both of which are essential for maintaining a healthy nervous system and for the formation of cells.

Polyunsaturated fats can be sourced from various foods and are a good source of essential fatty acids (EFAs). These fats cannot be produced by your body. Eggs, flaxseeds and nuts provide a good source of these fats for vegetarians.

Monounsaturated fats (MUFAs) are also said to help lower blood cholesterol and protect the heart from disease. Nuts, avocados, olive and rapeseed oils are good sources of MUFAs.

Remember that becoming a vegetarian is not an instant health fix. Purely eating dairy products in place of meat or fish, or eating an excess of refined carbohydrates such as white bread and potatoes, pasta or rice is likely to lead to weight gain and, crucially, a lack of vital nutrients. Make sure that you are imaginative and creative in the kitchen, unleashing the full potential that the world of vegetarianism offers. The recipes contained in Chapter 5 will give you some great ideas and should set you on the road to a healthy heart and a happy stomach.

Pocket tip ✤

Vegetarian instant and processed foods can be just as unhealthy as meat versions due to the high levels of salt, fat and sugar – just because something is vegetarian doesn't mean it is automatically healthier.

The principles about limiting your intake of foods with a high fat content and exercising control over portion size also apply to vegetarians. It is possible to be a vegetarian and not eat meat but still overeat chocolate, cakes, biscuits and crisps; however, you wouldn't be very healthy and would be likely to be above your ideal body weight for your height. To lose weight or retain a healthy weight, you also need to exercise – walking, cycling, running or swimming, etc. Likewise, why not try to get outside and do some gardening? It means you can grow your own vegetables and be provided with a natural, inexpensive and satisfying store of delicious veg whilst you get some exercise in the garden.

ETHICAL AND RELIGIOUS DECISIONS

A healthy heart is nothing without a healthy mind and many vegetarians are engaged with political and religious causes based on strongly held principles. Often these principles can be the primary reason that someone embarks on a vegetarian lifestyle. Outlined below are some of the key issues which can encourage people to move towards changing their diet and their lifestyle.

Religious reasons

In many religions, eating certain types of meat is forbidden. For instance, in the Islamic and Jewish faiths the eating of pork is prohibited. Many religions which originated in India enshrine vegetarianism at their heart, such as Hinduism and Jainism. The principle of *ahimsa* (non-violence) extends to the animal world and encourages many followers to live as vegans or lacto-vegetarians.

Buddhism is another religion which commonly involves vegetarianism. Although eating meat is not forbidden for all Buddhists, attitudes vary by location. Experts estimate that roughly half of all Buddhists are vegetarian. Buddhist monks are forbidden from eating meat if they are aware it was killed specifically for them, although if they are given it as hospitality they are bound to accept.

Various Christian sects in America such as the Seventh Day Adventists and Church of Latter Day Saints, often abstain from eating meat. In these religions, the prohibition against the eating of animals is related to the taking of life. They simply believe that it is wrong to murder or kill anyone, whether it is a human or an animal.

Pocket tip ✤

The Society of Ethical and Religious Vegetarians is an inter-faith organisation which intends to unite those from different belief-sets in their shared choice of lifestyle. Looking on their website will guide you to interesting discussions and information about the role of vegetarianism in religion (www.serv-online.org).

Animal rights and animal welfare

Many people decide to become a vegetarian because they feel that eating meat is unethical and believe that the slaughter process is cruel. Becoming a vegetarian for ethical reasons remains a common and popular reason in the Western world, as advances in modern technology in broadcast and media have helped supporters spread the word and educate people about the methods used in animal farming and slaughter.

Some vegetarians argue that the slaughter of animals can never be humane. Whilst in most Western countries animals must be slaughtered following strict legal guidelines to ensure welfare, there have been animal cruelty cases exposed throughout the years. More recently it has been factory farming – the process of rearing livestock in confinement in a high stocking density – that has come under the spotlight. *Hugh's Chicken Run* featuring celebrity chef Hugh Fearnley-Whittingstall documented the often cruel conditions of chicken battery farming operations in the UK.

Pocket fact

Almost three quarters of shoppers told an RSPCA survey that they had changed what they bought because of recent campaigns to highlight cruelty in the poultry industry. The RSPCA also state that nearly a third of Europeans are buying less meat as a result of welfare concerns.

If you are interested in finding out about the ethical and moral dilemmas of eating meat, then it is well worth reading New York author Jonathan Safran Foer's 2009 book *Eating Animals*. His investigation of the contrast between animal rights and animal welfare raises interesting issues about slaughterhouses, wastefulness and the health impact of eating meat. In an online article, film star Natalie Portman claimed that the book turned her from 'from a 20-year vegetarian to a vegan activist'.

Animal Welfare means that all animals used by humans need to have their basic needs met regarding health, housing and food, and that they don't experience unnecessary suffering when providing for human needs. Animal welfare differs from the movement for animal rights, however. Whilst those who believe in animal welfare make allowances for the responsible use of animals by humans, those who campaign for animal rights reject any use of animals as exploitation. People's stance in this debate can often inform whether they follow a vegetarian or vegan lifestyle.

Environmental reasons

Environmental vegetarians believe that animal production methods such as intensive agriculture are environmentally unsustainable and are a key factor in global warming. This is because of the amount of fossil fuels, water and energy that farming requires, alongside the methane produced by livestock, which contributes to greenhouse gases. The *Guardian* estimates that food production is responsible for 15% to 20% of the UK's greenhouse gas emissions. Methane gas has 25 times the global warming impact of carbon dioxide and a single cow can produce an incredible 500 litres of methane a day! From an environmental standpoint, it requires less land, money, and energy to produce foods for a vegetarian diet; for example producing one calorie from animal protein releases 11 times as much carbon dioxide as required for one calorie from plant protein.

Likewise, the clearing of forests to allow for animal pasture has damaged the world's forest stock. In the Brazilian Amazon, the principal reason for deforestation has been the expansion of cattle ranching as the country's development drives an increased appetite for a meat-rich diet. Clearing forests diminishes the planet's ability to process carbon dioxide and is widely linked to the worsening of global warming.

Sustainability is one of the largest issues driving environmental vegetarianism. If the world's population continues to develop then current dietary trends cannot be sustained. The United Nations Environment Program's (UNEP) International Panel of Sustainable

Resource Management, stated in a recent report that a worldwide move towards a vegan diet was crucial for ensuring concerns like global hunger, fuel poverty and climate change were lessened.

Pocket fact 📌

Studies have suggested that animal farming contributes significantly to global warming, and in 2009, the UK Climate Chief Lord Stern appealed to the British public to give up eating meat to help reduce the rise in greenhouse gases.

FINANCIAL REASONS

Following a vegetarian diet is not only better for your health, your morals and the environment but also for your wallet! It is no surprise that the highest rates of vegetarianism in the world are in developing countries, where access to different food types is often limited. Yet such frugality can be an excellent spur to improve your diet with inexpensive and healthy vegetables in a country awash with cheap junk food. If you swap the red meat, poultry and fish in your diet with vegetarian alternatives you'll find plant proteins are much cheaper than the equivalent amount of animal protein.

Many turn towards economic vegetarianism in pursuit of a more simple life. This desire is often allied to religious or political beliefs and driven by the recognition of conflicting 'wants' and 'needs'. Self-sufficiency can be one of the most satisfying ways to develop this simple life and reject consumerism. Living a simple life places a higher value on spirituality, values and health than on fulfilling your expected economic function in modern society. Figures like the Buddha, John the Baptist, Leo Tolstoy and Gandhi were notable champions of the virtue of the simple life.

Money saving tips

Here are a few practical tips on how to save money with a vegetarian or mostly vegetarian diet.

Think big

- Buy vegetarian staple foods in bulk. It is generally cheaper to buy larger packs of goods such as dried beans, rice, oats, and grains than pre-prepared, ready-to-eat meals. Dried goods will last a long time if stored correctly, generally in an air-tight container in a cool, dry place.

- Supermarkets often offer 'buy two get one free' discounts, so if you have room in your freezer it is worth stocking up.

- Learn what times of the day your supermarket discounts fresh produce such as fruit and vegetables to snap up a few bargains. A slightly squashed or overripe vegetable can easily be used in a homemade soup or stew.

- Cook dishes in bulk to eat for lunch the next day or freeze the remainder to have a healthy ready meal when you are short of time.

Think local

- It is often cheaper to shop at local markets where you are also likely to get fresher, better quality fruit and vegetables.

- Get online and find out what's happening near you with the Vegetarian Society (www.vegsoc.org). Many vegetarians like to help out others beginning to follow the lifestyle. There may be local meetings, cooperative food groups or exchanges. If there isn't, why not start one?

Think personal

- Try growing your own vegetables if you have a garden. If not, why not try growing some salad greens in a pot? It is a satisfying and inexpensive way of producing food.

- It is cheaper to make meals from scratch rather than buying prepared vegetarian meals or alternatives and it gives you a chance to experiment.

Pocket fact 🌶

In 2010 The Daily Telegraph *reported that the cost of buying red meat in the UK had shot up a whopping 10% over the last three years, with bacon close behind at 9%. This was due to the surge in the cost of fossil fuels and grain needed to feed livestock.*

GENERAL DISLIKE OF MEAT

Last, but not least, is the simplest reason to give up eating meat. Not everyone who wants to cut meat out of their diet is concerned with broader issues of conscience, health or religion. Many people simply do not like the texture or flavour of meat.

Pocket fact 🌶

In 2010 there were 3.7 million vegetarians in Britain.

🥕 FIRST STEPS TO BECOMING 🥕 A VEGETARIAN

It's important to consider exactly why you want to become a vegetarian, as keeping this in mind will help steel your resolve to live a healthier life. Although vegetarianism can be a useful aid for weight loss, many of its benefits won't be seen unless you stick to the diet in the long-term. Lifestyle changes do require motivation, so make sure you are firm in your convictions. Think about why you want to become vegetarian, and make sure that you believe in your goal.

DOING IT YOUR WAY

It is important to remember that there is no right or wrong way to becoming a vegetarian. It's a personal decision and it's your body, so take whatever steps you feel comfortable with, at whatever pace you want.

If you have a friend or family member who is a vegetarian, chatting to them about their experiences as a vegetarian can be a good place to start. They are likely to be able to offer support and reassurance as you take your first steps towards vegetarianism.

So, if you would like to become a vegetarian, but feel nervous or apprehensive, remember it's normal to feel like this. Even if eating meat was a big part of your life, rest assured within time you will learn to love your new diet.

THINKING ABOUT YOUR FOOD CUPBOARD

A useful thing to do prior to starting your vegetarian diet – or if you feel your existing vegetarian diet has become slightly stale – is to make a list of the foods you regularly eat for breakfast, lunch and dinner, including any snacks or desserts. Next write down the ingredients found in each dish.

Finally think about what vegetarian alternatives are available for these ingredients – just check in your local health food store or supermarket if you're unsure – you may be surprised to find most ingredients are easily available. The growing popularity of vegetarianism has resulted in a greater selection of substitutes on the market.

Keep an eye out for the following alternatives to meat or animal products to help you adapt to your new diet.

- **Alcoholic drinks.** Not all wines, beers or spirits are vegetarian as animal products are used to enhance flavour or as part of the distilling process. However vegetarian-friendly drinks are readily available so there's no need to go tee-total. See p.56 on vegetarian wine and beer for tips.

- **Bacon.** This can be replaced by soya-based bacon strips.

- **Biscuits.** These can be bought or made without eggs or dairy products.

- **Burgers.** These can be replaced with nut, bean, vegetable, soya or Quorn alternatives that are readily available and taste great.

- **Butter.** This is easily replaced by dairy-free margarine or in baking by oil.

- **Cakes.** These can be made with dairy-free, egg-free mixes and soya milks.

- **Cheese.** This can be replaced by soya- or rice-based cheese. Many vegetarians don't realise that the rennet (an enzyme used when making cheese) found in some cheeses isn't vegetarian so do watch out for this.

- **Chocolate.** You can get chocolate without dairy.

- **Eggs.** These can be substituted with mashed tofu or dried egg substitutes. When baking cakes, mashed banana works well.

- **Gelatine.** This is protein obtained by boiling animal bones, tendons, ligaments, hooves and/or skin. It is a common ingredient in jelly sweets, set yogurts, cheesecakes and long-life drinks. Alternatives include agar-agar, fruit pectin, and locust bean gum.

- **Ham.** This can even be replaced with soya substitute meat slices.

- **Ice cream.** This is easily replaced by soya- or rice-based frozen desserts. Freedoms (www.worthenshaws-freedom.co.uk) is a new brand that appeared on *Dragons' Den*; it is dairy-free and tastes great.

- **Mayonnaise.** This is easily replaced by egg-free or tofu-based alternatives.

- **Milk.** Replace with soya milk, rice milk, nut or oat milk.

- **Mince.** This can be replaced with soya products that have a similar texture and appearance when cooked.

- **Sausages.** These can be replaced by soya/tofu sausage.

- **Steak.** Replace this with soya versions.

- **Yogurt.** This can be replaced by soya yogurt. Several brands are now available, such as Alpro, Provamel and Sojade.

See Chapter 4 for advice on vegetarian alternatives and see p.166 for a list of vegan alternatives.

TAKING IT SLOWLY

For many people the steps towards becoming a vegetarian can involve reducing the amount of meat they eat gradually or by increasing the number of meat-free days they have. Others prefer to opt for a gradual reduction of meat; for example, they may first stop eating red meats such as beef or lamb, then white meat such as chicken, and finally fish.

Pocket tip ✣

While there are many benefits to being a vegetarian, not everyone who attempts to adopt this lifestyle succeeds. Make a list of why becoming a vegetarian is important to you and tape it to your fridge or bathroom mirror to remind you why it's worthwhile persisting.

Meat-free Monday

If you want to give vegetarianism a go, but aren't ready to go the whole hog (excuse the pun) then taking part in the Meat Free Monday (MFM) campaign is a good way to test out a vegetarian diet. Supported by Sir Paul McCartney and daughters Stella and Mary, the campaign has helped publicise the negative environmental and health implications of eating meat.

Continuing the pioneering vegetarian legacy of Paul's wife Linda McCartney, who died of breast cancer in 1998, the campaign emphasises that giving up eating meat just one day a week can have health benefits, help reduce the effect on global warming caused by cattle rearing, and can help save money. For more information and great recipe ideas visit www.meatfreemondays.com.

While giving up all red meat, poultry and fish in one go is great if it suits you, don't be afraid to take it slowly and give your body chance to get used to potentially new foods and cope without meat.

ALL IN ONE GO

Some people will prefer to give up all meat and fish at once. While this takes a little more determination and planning than the gradual transition to vegetarianism, it's not impossible and many vegetarians have followed this approach. Like giving up any habit, it can be hard, but if you have the will power to do it then anything is possible.

If you decide to give up meat and fish in one go then it is worth preparing yourself by taking stock of your food cupboards — remove anything that contains meat or fish that could tempt you in the event of a momentary lapse. You may need to carefully read the labels of certain products to check whether they contain gelatine or any other animal by-products.

ADVICE FOR THE EARLY STAGES

WHAT TO DO IF YOU SLIP UP

If you can't resist temptation and eat meat during the early stages of your transition to vegetarianism or have the occasional slip don't beat yourself up or give up. It can take a little time before your body stops craving meat if it is a food you used to eat regularly.

PLAN AHEAD – AVOID AWKWARD SITUATIONS AND DON'T GO HUNGRY!

A bit of simple planning can save embarrassment and prevent you going hungry! One mistake new vegetarians often make is that when they are eating out, they don't think of what they might have to eat. Most dinner party hosts will have no problem making a vegetarian option, or cooking the meat separately from the rest of the meal, provided they are given a bit of warning. Going to a party or a dinner can also be a good way to introduce your friends to a bit of vegetarian cooking if you make a great dish and take it along. See p.107 for more on this.

TRY OUT NEW RECIPES – AND CREATE YOUR OWN

Finding and planning vegetarian recipes is half of the battle and when you have cracked the art of vegetarian cooking the possibilities are endless. To help create greater variety in your diet and avoid boredom try cooking one new dish a week and create your own cookbook of your favourites. For more information on cooking as a vegetarian, refer to the recipes and cooking tips in Chapter 5.

MAKE IT FUN

Most importantly, have fun becoming a vegetarian. It is important not to confuse a vegetarian diet with a restrictive eating plan which deprives you of all treats. A vegetarian diet shouldn't feel like punishment and if it does you're doing something wrong, and are less likely to stick to your new diet if you view it that way.

Depending on the type of vegetarianism you have chosen to follow you can still have the odd treat and experiment with new recipes, so live a little and reward yourself for becoming a vegetarian, as the odd piece of chocolate or cake or glass of wine won't hurt. Have fun and feel proud of all you have achieved, after all it has been well earned!

Pocket tip ❧

If you already have vegetarian friends or family, spend time with them and enjoy eating out or cooking at home. They will best understand the challenges of becoming a vegetarian and offer support if you need it.

CONVINCING FRIENDS AND FAMILY

While you may be excited about your new vegetarian diet, your family and friends may require a little convincing. One thing to remember is not to pressure your friends and family into also choosing vegetarianism, rather to inform them why you have chosen it.

ALLAYING HEALTH WORRIES

One reason your friends and family may appear unsupportive of your vegetarian diet could be because they are worried about the impact it will have on your health. Many non-vegetarians have the misconception that a vegetarian diet is lacking in protein and iron – although thankfully this is not true.

It is important to discuss any health worries your friends and family have by showing them you have followed nutritional advice and are eating sensibly as a vegetarian. It may also be worth reminding them that you know how to get all the essential nutrients your body requires and mention the following health benefits.

Five facts that show a vegetarian diet is healthy

1. Reduced cholesterol.

2. Lower blood pressure.

3. Less likely to be obese or overweight.

4. Lower risk of developing diseases such as cancer, heart disease, stroke and diabetes.

5. Better digestive health: a vegetarian diet is high in fibre, which is beneficial for the digestive system.

CHAT ABOUT IT

Take the time to sit down and discuss with friends and family why you have chosen to become a vegetarian and why it is so important to you. They may not have realised how you feel about it and may surprise you by being supportive and understanding.

DON'T TRY TO CONVERT THEM

Some vegetarians become so sure that their diet is best that they forget it may not be for everyone. It is important to accept that vegetarianism won't suit some people and remember that if we all had the same opinions and beliefs the world would be a very boring place. Don't try to convert people, just try to get them to accept your point of view.

LESSENING THE IMPACT ON THEIR LIFE

If you are the only vegetarian in your family or group of friends it can create a challenge for them as they will have to cook or shop slightly differently for you – or vice versa. One way you could help is by offering to share the cooking and buy in your own veg-etarian alternatives if necessary to avoid them having to struggle thinking about how to cater for you.

The best way to convince family and friends that a vegetarian diet is healthy, nutritious and most importantly delicious is through their stomachs. Offer to cook a vegetarian option along with a meat option or try adapting a classic dish such as lasagne or spaghetti Bolognese to show them that vegetarian cooking can be varied, exciting and tastes good!

Top ten vegetarian options to offer

1. *Roasted vegetable lasagne with salad and garlic bread.*
2. *Vegetable pizza.*
3. *Lentil dhal with rice and naan bread.*
4. *Baked cheese fondue with French bread and vegetable dips.*
5. *Vegetable Thai green curry.*
6. *Three-bean chilli with nachos.*
7. *Creamy mushroom risotto.*
8. *Bean burgers with potato wedges and salad.*
9. *Soya mince cottage pie with roast vegetables.*
10. *Vegetable and noodle stir fry with vegetable spring rolls.*

PUTTING UP WITH JOKES AND JIBES

It is likely that from time to time people will react negatively to your diet choice. Dedicated meat-eaters often enjoy making fun of vegetarians, regarding them as the light-weights of the culinary world or as a soft, tree-hugging pushover.

'You don't know what you're missing out on' is an oft-heard comment from non-vegetarians who can't understand how anyone could live without meat – or choose not to eat it. Rather than getting into a heated health debate with non-vegetarians it can sometimes be better and easier just to make a joke out of it. Politely point out that yes you do know what you're missing out on – an increased chance of not fitting into your favourite jeans and high cholesterol!

SUPPORT FORUMS AND ORGANISATIONS TO JOIN

If you are new to vegetarianism these forums can help you through the early stages and continue to be useful tools later.

THE VEGETARIAN SOCIETY (WWW.VEGSOC.ORG)

The Vegetarian Society is a registered charity which presents news, recipes, an events calendar and educational material about vegetarianism.

This is an excellent place to look for inspiration, support and search for delicious vegetarian recipes. The website also hosts an online community forum that users can join free of charge and use to interact with others.

Pocket fact

The Vegetarian Society was founded in Britain in 1847 and is the world's oldest vegetarian society.

THE VEGETARIAN & VEGAN FOUNDATION (VVF) (WWW.VEGETARIAN.ORG.UK)

The Vegetarian & Vegan Foundation (VVF) is a registered charity that monitors and explains scientific research linking diet to health, helping people to make an informed choice about what they eat.

VEGETARIAN RECIPE CLUB (WWW.VEGETARIANRECIPECLUB.ORG.UK)

The Vegetarian Recipe Club is the sister website of the VVF and is a free resource for vegetarians and vegans to find and share vegetarian and vegan recipes. If you want to receive the recipe binder by post there is an additional charge. The group sends out a weekly newsletter filled with lots of fun and tasty new recipes.

🥕 TEN FAMOUS VEGETARIANS 🥕 IN HISTORY

Here are 10 famous vegetarians to inspire you.

1. **Plato, 428–347BC**. Often regarded as the father of vegetarianism, the Greek philosopher Plato believed that eating meat distressed the animal spirit. In his work *The Laws*, Plato noted a link between human behaviour and dietary choices.

2. **Pythagoras, 570–495BC**. Pythagoras was a Greek philosopher and mathematician, who along with creating the infamous mathematical equation 'Pythagoras Theorem' was a forefather of vegetarianism. The term the 'Pythagorean diet' became synonymous with an avoidance of the flesh of slaughtered animals and was used before the term vegetarianism was coined. Pythagoras's ethics called for followers to abstain from 'harsh-sounding bloodshed', in particular animal sacrifice, and 'never to eat meat'.

3. **Leonardo da Vinci, 1452–1519.** Known throughout history as a great artist and a leading figure in the Renaissance movement, da Vinci's views have been documented in his art

and in his notebooks and he questioned not just the morality of eating animals but also debated whether eating meat was necessary for health.

4. **Sir Isaac Newton, 1643–1727.** Newton was a physicist, mathematician, philosopher, astronomer and theologian who studied light, motion and gravity. He was convinced that eating a vegetarian diet was healthiest.

5. **Benjamin Franklin, 1706–1790.** One of the founding fathers of America and acclaimed inventor, Benjamin Franklin believed that a vegetarian diet could improve his mind while also benefiting him financially as during colonial times, meat was expensive and generally regarded as a luxury.

6. **William Blake, 1757–1827.** Blake was a poet, artist and printmaker, labelled controversial largely because of his unconventional and radical attacks on religion. He followed and advocated a vegetarian diet.

7. **Percy Bysshe Shelley, 1792–1822.** Widely regarded as one of the major English Romantic poets and as an unconventional thinker at the time, Shelley's views on idealism, free love, atheism and vegetarianism were considered radical in his day. Shelley was one of the first to speak out against the maltreatment of animals as he considered the slaughter of animals for food immoral. Shelley argued that the adoption of a vegetarian diet and the cessation of animal slaughter would put an end to social injustices such as poverty, crime, aggression, capitalism and war. Shelley also wrote several essays about vegetarianism including *On the Vegetable System of Diet* and *A Vindication of Natural Diet* in 1813 in which he wrote: 'If the use of animal food be, in consequence, subversive to the peace of human society, how unwarrantable is the injustice and the barbarity which is exercised toward these miserable victims.'

8. **Leo Tolstoy, 1828–1910.** Tolstoy was a novelist, philosopher, peace campaigner and humanitarian. Tolstoy wrote several essays and speeches on vegetarianism and animal cruelty. *The Vegetarian* was written in 1889 shortly after his

conversion to vegetarianism following a visit to a slaughter-house. Tolstoy wrote: 'As long as there are slaughterhouses, there will be battlefields.' Tolstoy lived very simply on bread, porridge, fruits and vegetables.

9. **Vincent Van Gogh, 1853–1890.** Van Gogh is highly regarded as one of the greatest post-impressionist artists. According to records of his letters, Van Gogh, like Tolstoy, became a vegetarian after visiting a slaughterhouse. He also stated that it was not necessary for people to eat meat every day.

10. **Albert Einstein, 1879–1955.** Awarded the Nobel Prize in 1921 for his work in physics, the German-born physicist gained American citizenship in 1940. It is unknown exactly how many years Einstein followed a vegetarian diet; however, it is clear that in the later years of his life he was a vegetarian. He said: 'Nothing will benefit human health and increase chances of survival for life on earth as much as the evolution to a vegetarian diet.'

Pocket fact

Shelley's wife, Mary Shelley, the acclaimed writer and author of the novel Frankenstein *(1818), made the famous character of Frankenstein's creature vegetarian. The creature says: 'My food is not that of man; I do not destroy the lamb and kid to glut my appetite; acorns and berries afford my sufficient nourishment.'*

TEN MODERN-DAY VEGETARIANS

Proving that vegetarianism is both healthy and cool is this bunch of well-known celebrity vegetarians.

1. Paul McCartney, musician.

2. Stella McCartney, fashion designer.

3. Joanna Lumley, actress.

4. Leona Lewis, musician.

5. Judi Dench, actress.

6. Natalie Portman, actress.

7. Ian McKellen, actor.

8. Pamela Anderson, actress and model.

9. Forest Whitaker, actor.

10. Morrissey, musician.

Pocket fact 🖋

The former Smiths' frontman Morrissey has been a vegetarian since his childhood. In fact he is so passionate about vegetarianism and animal rights that he banned meat from being served at all the venues he played at during his 2011 UK tour.

2

NUTRITIONAL INFORMATION

A common myth surrounding vegetarian nutrition is that vegetarians are lacking in protein and other nutrients. In fact, it is extremely unlikely that a healthy vegetarian eating a wholesome and nutritious vegetarian diet will be lacking in protein or any other essential nutrient. This chapter looks at the nutritional needs of vegetarians and provides useful tips so you can ensure that you have a balanced and, most importantly, varied diet that you enjoy eating.

Note

It is important that you take the advice of your doctor before changing your diet. Always consult your general practitioner (GP) if you have any queries or concerns, or if you have any medical conditions which may need to be taken into account.

OVERVIEW OF DIETARY REQUIREMENTS

Getting your daily dose of vitamins and minerals isn't that hard on a vegetarian diet as long as you incorporate as wide a range of fruits, vegetables, pulses, and wholegrain into your diet as possible.

Essential nutrients are important in helping your body perform different functions such as:

- promoting growth
- repairing tissues

- regulating heat
- supporting body processes.

A lack of essential nutrients can lead to lethargy, tiredness or a weak immune system, which can further lead to a tendency to pick up bugs and leave you susceptible to feeling the cold.

The five nutrients that vegetarians may lack if a healthy diet isn't followed are:

- vitamin D
- vitamin B12
- iron
- selenium
- omega-3 fatty acids.

However, it is very easy to get enough of these in a vegetarian diet, provided you eat the right foods.

As your body can't make essential nutrients on its own, you need to ensure that your diet contains the recommended daily allowance (RDA) of these essential nutrients to keep your body and mind healthy and active.

VITAMINS

Vitamin A

Vitamin A, also known as retinol, has several essential functions which include keeping the eyes healthy and protecting vision and strengthening the immune system. It's also good for the skin.

Vegetarians can get vitamin A from these foods:

- green leafy vegetables
- carrots
- dairy products such as cheese, milk and yogurt or soya alternatives

- eggs
- tomatoes
- grapefruit
- pecan nuts.

Vitamin B1

Vitamin B1, also known as thiamine, is good for the nervous system, heart, muscles and for digestion. It also helps other B vitamins to break down and release energy from food.

This vitamin can be found in an abundance of vegetarian foods, so here is just a short list:

- dairy, such as milk and cheese
- eggs
- vegetables
- fruit
- wholegrains
- peanuts (try to avoid heavily salted or roasted and stick to plain).

Vitamin B2

Vitamin B2, also known as riboflavin, is excellent for keeping your skin, nails, hair and eyes healthy and bright. It also supports the nervous system, aids digestion and helps the body create red blood cells.

Good sources of vitamin B2 are:

- milk
- eggs
- rice
- green leafy vegetables

- mushrooms
- fortified breakfast cereals
- yeast or a yeast extract product such as Marmite.

Vitamin B12

Vitamin B12 is the main vitamin vegetarians may lack as it is naturally present in meat and animal products. If you eat dairy or eggs it is unlikely that you will be deficient in B12, but if you follow a vegan or non-dairy vegetarian diet you may need to take a good-quality vitamin supplement or eat fortified foods and drinks to ensure you are getting enough.

Vitamin B12 is vital for growth and repair as it helps the body to release energy from food. It is also good for blood as it helps make red blood cells and keeps the nervous system healthy.

Good sources of B12 for vegetarians include:

- dairy such as milk, cheese and yogurts or fortified soya products
- eggs
- fortified yeast extract such as Marmite or similar
- fortified breakfast cereals
- quality B12 food supplement.

Pocket fact

A lack of vitamin B12 leads to a kind of anaemia in which the body produces abnormally large red blood cells, which stops them functioning properly. Symptoms of anaemia are a lack of energy and fatigue, which if left untreated can be serious.

Vitamin C

Vitamin C, also known as ascorbic acid, is great for the immune system and fighting infection, which is why it is often recommended to increase your vitamin C dose during illness. It also helps lower cholesterol and helps wounds heal faster as it supports tissue maintenance and growth.

The good news is vegetarians are likely to have plenty of vitamin C in their diet as it's found in a wide variety of fruits and vegetables. Good sources include:

- citrus fruits, in particular kiwis and oranges
- green vegetables
- peppers
- sweet potatoes
- fruit juices
- berries
- tomatoes.

Pocket fact 🌶

The body can't store vitamin C, so it is important that you include foods rich in vitamin C in your daily diet. Adults need around 40mg a day.

Vitamin D

Vitamin D is important for healthy bones and teeth. It also helps to regulate the amount of calcium in the body. A lack of vitamin D can lead to a condition known as rickets, which causes the bones to soften and weaken. Bow-shaped legs are common in people with acute rickets. Vitamin D also helps the body balance the amount of vitamin A it absorbs, as too much vitamin A can be harmful.

For vegetarians, the best sources of vitamin D are:

- dairy such as milk, cheese and yogurt, or soya alternatives
- eggs

- fortified breakfast cereals

- mushrooms

- fortified fruit juices.

The sun is also a good source of vitamin D as the skin's reaction to being in the sun causes vitamin D to form under the skin. This doesn't mean you should sit out in the sun for hours or allow yourself to burn; just 10–15 minutes a day should be long enough.

Pocket fact 🌶
The body can store surplus vitamin D for future use so you may not need it in your diet every day.

Vitamin E

Vitamin E helps protect the body's cells against toxins. It is also excellent for healthy and clear skin, which is why many cosmetic face creams contain this vitamin.

Vegetarians are likely to eat plenty of vitamin E as it is found in the following vegetarian favourites:

- nuts and seeds

- soya beans

- green vegetables

- eggs

- wholegrains

- wheat germ – often found in breakfast cereals.

Similarly to vitamin D, any excess of vitamin E is cleverly stored by the body for future use, so don't worry if you don't eat it every day.

Folic acid

In its natural state folic acid is known as folate and is good for the blood and for pregnant women as it helps limit the risk of central nervous system defects in unborn babies.

It is a good idea for pregnant vegetarian women, in particular, to make sure they are getting enough folic acid by eating:

- green leafy vegetables, in particular broccoli and curly kale

- peas

- asparagus

- chickpeas

- brown rice

- wholewheat bread

- yeast or yeast extract spread.

MINERALS

Iron

Iron is an essential mineral that helps the body produce red blood cells, which carry oxygen around the body. This mineral is good for the blood and muscles and vegetarians can get their daily dose of iron from the following foods:

- green leafy vegetables such as spinach, watercress, curly kale and broccoli

- dried fruits such as apricots and figs

- fortified breakfast cereals – try to opt for less sugary cereals

- wholemeal bread

- pulses.

The body cannot easily absorb iron without vitamin C, which helps the process. Try to mix iron and vitamin C-rich foods together in the same meal. For example, include steamed spinach with pulses in a light curry, or drink a glass of orange juice with your meal.

Women's iron needs

Women need more iron than men: an average adult woman needs 14.8mg of iron per day, while an average adult man needs only 8.7mg per day. This is because of the iron lost in blood during menstruation.

A lack of iron is known as anaemia and can cause serious medical problems if untreated. Symptoms can include tiredness, general weakness, a pale skin colour, headaches, depression and low immunity.

Vegetarian women can get their daily iron requirements from eating green leafy vegetables such as spinach and broccoli, pulses and fortified breakfast cereals. A good-quality iron supplement can also be taken if necessary.

Calcium

Calcium is an essential mineral that helps build and maintain strong bones, healthy teeth and good kidney function. It also helps regulate the health of the immune system.

Calcium can be found in the following vegetarian foods:

- milk and dairy products such as cheese and yogurt
- nuts and seeds
- leafy green vegetables
- pulses and legumes such as kidney beans and lentils
- wholegrains
- tofu
- orange juice.

Potassium

Potassium helps to maintain a healthy pH level in our body's fluids. It also helps regulate the functions of the heart and kidney, blood pressure, bone mass, muscle growth and also supports the nervous system. Adults need 3,500mg of potassium a day.

Pocket fact 🌶

A lack of potassium can result in the condition called hypokalaemia; symptoms include an increase in blood pressure, muscle weakness and a general sense of tiredness. It can also put a strain on the heart.

Good sources of potassium for vegetarians include:

- bananas
- avocados
- dried or fresh apricots
- potatoes – white and sweet
- raisins
- pumpkin.

Magnesium

Magnesium plays a key role in the formation and maintenance of healthy bones. Along with calcium, magnesium is important to maintain bone density and help guard against conditions such as osteoporosis, where the bones thin down, becoming brittle and breaking more easily.

Pocket fact 🌶

Elderly people, women who have gone through menopause and very underweight people are at risk of developing osteoporosis.

Vegetarian foods that are high in magnesium include:

- milk and yogurt
- green leafy vegetables
- wholewheat
- raisins
- pulses
- brazil nuts
- artichokes.

Exercise is also recommended as it helps keep the bones strong.

Zinc

Zinc is good for the immune system and helps the body make new cells and enzymes which help wounds heal faster. It also boosts the libido and helps men produce a healthy sperm count.

Some zinc-rich vegetarian foods are:

- dairy such as milk and cheese
- brown rice
- wholegrains
- fortified cereals
- pumpkin seeds
- beans
- potatoes.

Selenium

Vegetarians need to ensure they get enough selenium as it helps keep the immune system strong and is good for liver function.

Try adding these selenium-rich foods into your diet:

- brazil nuts
- eggs

- wholewheat bread

- watercress

- cheese

- sunflower seeds

- peas

- mangos.

Pocket tip ⚜

Keep a packet of dried nuts and seeds in your bag to snack on, or sprinkle some on your morning porridge, to keep your selenium levels topped up.

CARBOHYDRATES

Carbohydrates are often unfairly criticised and treated as a sinful food as many diets advocate ditching the 'carbs' to help weight loss. In fact, carbohydrates provide a major source of energy and should make up approximately 40%–50% of your daily diet. The vegetarian diet should be rich in wholegrain and wheat carbohydrates.

The two types of carbohydrates are known as complex and simple, often dubbed 'good' and 'bad' carbs.

Simple carbohydrates

Simple – 'bad' – carbohydrates, also known as simple sugars, are fast-release carbohydrates that can be broken down and released into the body to produce energy quickly; however, simple carbohydrates can cause blood sugar levels to dip quickly too.

Sources of simple carbohydrates include:

- fructose (fruit) sugar, mangos and pineapples are high in fructose

- cakes
- biscuits
- sweets
- fizzy drinks
- white bread, pasta and rice.

White bread *v.* brown bread

White bread is made with wheat flour which has had the bran (husk) and germ removed. Removing these gives white bread a lighter colour, but also most of the nutritional goodness as this is contained in the bran and germ. This means the end product is lower in zinc, fibre and all the other beneficial fats and nutrients but much higher in simple carbohydrates.

After the baker has removed the bran and germ, the bread flour is bleached, involving some nasty chemicals and a refining process. These chemicals do you no good and take extra energy to produce, ensuring that white bread remains less environmentally friendly.

Watch out for brown bread which has been processed in the same way. The easiest way is to look at the ingredient list. Flour should be the greatest ingredient by volume and the presence of things like 'caramel' tell you that the bread's colouring has been enhanced.

Natural brown bread has more fibre, is wholewheat, encourages the body to release sugar more slowly from complicated carbohydrates and is less likely to lead to problems with cholesterol (it contains a different density of cholesterol which is better for you). It doesn't seem too much of a contest!

Complex carbohydrates

Complex – 'good' – carbohydrates take longer to be digested, so glucose is released into the blood more slowly, helping to maintain a stable energy source rather than the fast burst of the simple carbohydrate.

Sources of good carbohydrates for vegetarians include:

- wholewheat pasta
- brown rice
- noodles
- wholegrain or granary bread
- potatoes
- fruit
- vegetables.

Our body needs to get enough carbohydrates to function properly and keep us healthy and active. Vegetarians should eat a balance of simple and complex carbohydrates with a focus on wholegrains and vegetables.

Pocket tip ⚜

Adults need on average around 2 litres of liquids a day to stay hydrated and for the body functions to perform efficiently. Tea, coffee and alcohol don't count towards this target as they act as a diuretic (a substance which causes an increased passing of urine), causing the body to lose water.

PROTEIN

Protein is good for hair, skin and nails. In fact, protein forms a major component of all of our cells, and getting enough protein is fundamental to good health. Proteins provide around 15% of dietary energy and are needed for growth and repair.

Proteins are made up of amino acids (which help cell development, repair tissues and support the immune system) and while animal meat does contain a decent source, contrary to popular belief, the vegetarian diet is not lacking in protein.

Good vegetarian sources of protein include:

- nuts and seeds
- beans, pulses and legumes
- eggs
- soya products
- mycoprotein
- tofu
- peanut butter
- quinoa
- mushrooms.

Pocket tip ⚜

Try spreading sugar-free peanut butter on two plain oatcakes for a mid-morning high protein and slow energy release snack.

ESSENTIAL FATTY ACIDS: OMEGA-3 AND OMEGA-6

It is important that vegetarians get enough omega-3 and omega-6, known as essential fatty acids, in their diets in order to maintain a healthy heart and reduce the risk of heart-related disease. Omega-3 and omega-6 fatty acids are commonly found in oily fish and eggs, but there are plenty of vegetarian alternatives that contain high doses such as:

- flaxseed oil
- rapeseed oil
- linseeds

- pumpkin seeds
- sunflower seeds
- soya
- walnuts and walnut oil
- canola oil
- sunflower oil.

Pocket tip ❧

For an easy way to incorporate omega-3 into your diet, sprinkle a mix of omega-3 seeds on your breakfast cereal, drizzle a little of an omega-rich oil on salad or use in cooking and snack on nuts regularly.

🥕 COMMON MYTHS ABOUT VEGETARIAN NUTRITION 🥕

It is quite likely that you will have heard or read the occasional negative comment about the health and safety of the vegetarian diet. The vast majority of these are myths and have been proven so by scientific studies into nutritional and diet needs.

MYTH: PROTEIN ONLY COMES FROM MEAT

Many people in the UK eat *more* protein than they actually need due to a meat-rich and high-fat diet. A study conducted by the American *National Institute of Health* in 2009 showed the consumption of red meat to be strongly linked to increases in mortality owing to cancer and heart disease. Likewise, the *Journal of the American Diabetic Association* published findings that measures of cardiovascular disease were being worsened by high animal protein diets but improved by vegetarian diets.

A whole host of animal-free foods contain good sources of protein and can help you meet your nutritional requirements in a healthy way. Men require around 55.5g of protein a day and women require 45g. Vegetarian adults can get all the protein they need by eating two or three servings of protein each day. A portion of protein could include:

- two eggs
- three tablespoons of seeds
- a handful of nuts
- one tablespoon of peanut butter
- ½ cup of tofu
- ½ tin of baked beans.

MYTH: VEGETARIANS ARE LACKING IN CALCIUM IF THEY DON'T EAT DAIRY

We probably all remember being told as a child to drink our milk if we wanted to grow big and tall and have strong bones. In fact, calcium can be found in a variety of plant-based and animal-free foods, so there is no reason that vegetarians who don't eat dairy or vegans should be lacking in calcium.

The Harvard School of Public Health recommends getting your daily fix of calcium from non-dairy sources such as baked beans, pak choi, fortified soya milk, spring greens, and supplements that contain both calcium and vitamin D (which is better than just calcium on its own).

MYTH: IRON ONLY COMES FROM RED MEAT

There has long been the myth that the vegetarian diet is lacking in iron. In fact, this is extremely unlikely to be the case.

There are two kinds of iron that can be found in the diet, known as haem iron and non-haem iron (think haemoglobin – the iron in your blood). Haem iron is only found in meat and non-haem is sourced from plant-based foods and is the main source of dietary iron. According to the Vegetarian Society, the general meat-eating population in the UK obtain only between 10% and 14% of their iron from meat while cereals, bread, fruit and vegetables provide 85% of dietary iron.

Popeye's love for the green stuff

The infamous cartoon sailor Popeye is famous for his love of a can of spinach before a fight for boosting his muscle power to superhuman levels. While spinach doesn't quite work like that for the rest of us, its iron content has helped it achieve notoriety as a superfood.

Researchers at the Karolinska Institute in Sweden recently discovered that the inorganic nitrate in spinach is the source of its strength-giving property. In the research, a group of exercising volunteers were each given a small dose of nitrate, equivalent to the amount found in a normal plate-sized portion of spinach. The researchers discovered that the nitrate helped to reduce the subjects' need for oxygen, which further helped to improve their muscular performance and efficiency.

Try to eat plenty of green leafy vegetables such as spinach, dried fruits and pulses to keep your iron stores topped up. Wash it all down with a glass of vitamin C-rich orange juice.

MYTH: VEGETARIANS ARE UNDERWEIGHT

Even though statistically vegetarians tend to be thinner than meat eaters (see p.6), it is quite easy to be overweight as a vegetarian if you don't eat healthily; after all tucking into large portions of chips, cheese, bread, pasta and junk food is technically vegetarian, but not very low fat or healthy!

On the other hand, eating a wholesome vegetarian diet does help people maintain a healthy weight and studies have shown that vegetarians are less likely to be overweight or obese. Vegetarians are only likely to be underweight if they are not eating enough calories for their height and level of activity.

Pocket tip ❧

If you are an underweight vegetarian and want to put on weight healthily try eating more foods rich in good fats such as avocados, bananas, nuts and seeds. Don't be tempted to skip meals and perhaps look to increase your portion size a little.

🥕 PREGNANT VEGETARIANS 🥕

Good nutrition is vital during pregnancy, and it is perfectly safe to continue with a vegetarian diet, provided a wholesome and balanced regime is followed.

According to the British Medical Association's 2009 report *Early Life Nutrition and Lifelong Health*: 'It is possible for vegetarians and vegans (people who eat no animal products at all, including dairy products) to be adequately nourished for successful pregnancy and lactation, but they need to be knowledgeable about nutrition and plan their diet carefully.' You can read the full report online by entering its title into an internet search engine.

Pocket tip ❧

Every pregnant woman may have slightly different nutritional requirements, so it is important to discuss with your GP or midwife if you have any concerns or questions, as this is just a brief guide.

Vegetarian pregnant women need to follow the same nutritional information as anyone else but should ensure they are receiving more of the following essential nutrients.

Iron

Pregnant women need more iron in their diet, particularly during the end stages of pregnancy as iron levels decrease (see p.32 for sources of iron-rich goods). If you are concerned about this, talk to a health professional, who may advise that you take an iron supplement during your pregnancy.

Pocket tip ✤

If you decide to take a vitamin or mineral supplement during your pregnancy check that the tablet shell is vegetarian as many contain gelatine. Most health food shops and pharmacies stock vegetarian supplements.

Calcium

More calcium is needed during pregnancy for the baby's developing bones. If you don't get enough calcium during pregnancy your body will start to supply the baby with calcium from your own bones so ovo-vegetarians and vegans who don't eat dairy need to take extra care to ensure they are getting enough calcium. For women who intend to breastfeed, taking a calcium supplement is advisable provided your GP or nurse gives you the go ahead.

Omega-3 fatty acids

It is important that plenty of omega-3-rich foods such as flaxseeds or flaxseed oils are eaten by pregnant vegetarians, as they play a vital role in the development of the baby's eyesight and brain function. Vegetarian flaxseed supplements are readily available.

Vitamin B12

Pregnant vegetarians may want to think about taking an additional supplement of B12 during their pregnancy as it is essential for the growth and development of the baby in the womb.

Folic acid

Pregnant vegetarians are unlikely to be lacking in folic acid as it is found in vegetables, fruit and wholegrain foods; however, it is worth monitoring your intake to be sure.

🥕 OLDER VEGETARIANS 🥕

As we age, our nutritional needs change and some foods may become less digestible. For elderly people it is perfectly safe and healthy to continue, or start, a vegetarian diet, but care must be taken to ensure that nutritional needs are met.

Older people are unlikely to have the ravenous appetite of a teenager, and indeed the appetite does reduce as we get older. However, it is important to eat properly as an elderly vegetarian in order to meet daily nutritional requirements, keep your energy levels topped up and avoid too much weight loss.

Pocket tip 🔱

Large meals or portions can be off-putting if your appetite is reduced. Try eating five small meals throughout the day or three small meals with two healthy snacks to help keep your calorie and nutrient intake up.

Older vegetarians' dietary needs aren't that radically different to younger vegetarians, but the body's ability to absorb vitamins and minerals decreases, so if you are an older vegetarian it is a good idea to eat more of these.

Calcium

The bones thin as we age and older women in particular are more at risk of developing osteoporosis meaning they should be eating plenty of green leafy vegetables, nuts and seeds, wholegrains and dairy or an alternative. It is often a good idea for older vegetarians to take a calcium supplement, but it is worth having a chat with your GP or health worker first.

Zinc, vitamins B6 and E

These are all excellent for boosting the immune system, which becomes less resistant to infections and viruses as we age. Eating more fruits and vegetables is helpful, as is taking a vitamin and mineral supplement to boost you stores and keep your body fighting fit.

Water

It is important that older vegetarians continue to drink plenty of liquids to keep hydrated. Dehydration can be common in older people and can lead to painful bladder or kidney infections that might need to be treated with antibiotics.

Pocket tip ❧

Older vegetarians may find that some foods become a little indigestible and can cause indigestion or flatulence. Eating natural yogurt or taking a Lactobacillus acidophilus *supplement to help these good bacteria in the gut can help.*

HELP AND SUPPORT FOR OLDER VEGETARIANS

Launched in 2008, the charity group Vegetarian for Life (www.vegetarianforlife.org.uk) provides excellent support and advice for older vegetarians. The group is funded by the Vegetarian Housing Association (VHA) and its main aim is to improve the quality of life for older vegetarians, vegans and their families.

🥕 DIABETIC VEGETARIANS 🥕

If you have diabetes, choosing a diet that helps stabilise your blood glucose levels is vital and a wholegrain vegetarian diet rich in fruit and vegetables, pulses and beans can help considerably.

The key to managing diabetes is adhering to a well-balanced vegetarian diet, where attention is paid to low fat, high fibres and high carbohydrates. This diet can be just as suitable for a diabetic as for anyone else.

For further advice visit www.diabetes.co.uk and discuss your plans with your doctor.

VEGETARIANS WITH FOOD ALLERGIES

Vegetarians with food allergies need to take care to avoid the food that causes a reaction. Food allergies can range from mild to severe and in some cases can be life-threatening. Common food allergies are caused by the following products:

- nuts and seeds
- soya
- gluten
- milk
- eggs.

It is important that you get tested by your doctor if you think you have a food allergy. If you are a vegetarian who doesn't eat dairy or eggs and you discover that you are allergic to soya or nuts you will need to boost your nutritional intake by eating other protein and nutritious foods, such as vegetables, fruits and pulses, grains and beans.

3

SHOPPING

Whilst vegetarianism can liven up your diet and improve your health, it can be difficult to break the habits of a lifetime when visiting the shops. This chapter is intended to serve as a guide for those wondering what to look for and where to buy the essential ingredients for a vegetarian lifestyle. Whether you are looking for alternatives to common foods which aren't vegetarian or trying to locate specialist stores and sites for more difficult to find items, this chapter will give you suggestions and guidance for how to shop veggie.

FOOD: VEGETARIAN ALTERNATIVES

From veggie bacon to soya milk to vegan breads and cakes, the shelves of supermarkets and shops are awash with great vegetarian food alternatives that fulfil even the hungriest vegetarian's nutritional needs. You will find that if you know where to look you can find everything you need to have a healthy vegetarian diet, without giving up the foods that you love.

MEAT ALTERNATIVES

While you may initially miss meat in your diet you may be surprised (and relieved) to discover that giving up meat can be much easier than you anticipated. If you previously enjoyed the taste and texture of meat there is no need to forgo sausages, burgers, mince or steak as there is now an excellent range of meat-free alternatives available. So if a meat craving hits, rest assured you can tuck into a burger or plate of sausage and mash when you feel the need – guilt free! Even those vegetarians who may not have previously enjoyed the taste or texture of meat, will find that meat alternatives can help add a little variety to your diet and provide a good source of protein without tasting really meaty.

Meat-free food market growth

Reports into the meat-free food markets show that there is a shift in the UK's eating habits as the value of the meat-free market has roughly doubled in the past decade. Mintel, the consumer and market report producer for the US, UK and Europe has published numerous studies on the growth in the meat-free product market.

Reports show that between 2007 and 2011, sales of vegetarian foods continued to grow between 6.2% and 6.9% per year. Furthermore, people who eat meat substitutes in the 15–24 age bracket are expected to increase in number by 1.4%, while among those aged 20–24 to the proportion increased by 7% in 2011.

Tofu

Tofu, unjustly, often receives criticism for being bland or tasteless. It is a well-known vegetarian and vegan protein that is often used in Asian cooking. It is made from soya bean curd and can be bought in a very soft form, known as silken, or in the more regular and sturdier form.

Often people think they dislike tofu because they haven't prepared or cooked it in a way that enhances its flavour and texture. When cooked correctly tofu can provide an excellent source of protein. It can also be included in meals subtly and doesn't need to form the basis of the meal. For example, you can try adding a couple of thinly sliced strips of tofu into a stir fry or salad. For more information on cooking with tofu, see p.77.

Pocket fact 🌶

Tofu is not only cheap, it's also low in fat (with no cholesterol), sugar and carbohydrates: 100g of uncooked tofu contains just 73 calories, of which 32 calories come from protein, 38 calories from fat and just 3 calories from carbohydrates. In comparison 100g of beef steak contains on average a whopping 225 calories.

Cauldron

Cauldron has been one of the UK's most important vegetarian food producers for over 30 years. Cauldron was born after founder Phillip Marshal took a trip across Asia where he discovered the process of making tofu from soya beans. Its tofu is one of the best selling brands and can be bought ready-marinated. Cauldron's range has now expanded since those early days to include products such as:

- falafel

- mushroom burgers

- pâtés such as sun-dried tomato or mushroom

- sausages

- ready meals.

For more information on Cauldron and for recipe ideas using its products, visit www.cauldronfoods.co.uk.

Mori-Nu

If you are looking for silken tofu in the UK, you will inevitably come across the Mori-Nu brand. Their firm, silken tofu is the best selling of that variety and is widely stocked in major supermarkets.

For more information on their range check www.morinu.com.

Mycoprotein

Mycoprotein is derived from a fungus and is used by most well-known vegetarian food brands to manufacture meat-free alternative foods. The mycoprotein is extracted from a fungus known as *Fusarium venenatum*, which is specifically grown in large vats to act as a meat alternative and high-protein food.

Mycoprotein is suitable for vegetarians who eat egg and dairy, as a small amount of egg white is used to bind it. As such, it is not a suitable alternative for those on more restrictive vegetarian or vegan diets. Make sure you always check the labels and ingredients first if you want to avoid these foods.

Quorn

Quorn is the leading brand of mycoprotein food in the UK, with products such as:

- scotch eggs
- mince
- beef slices
- sausages
- salmon-style fishcakes.

For more information on Quorn products and for recipe ideas, visit www.quorn.co.uk.

Pocket tip ❧

Most big UK supermarkets sell their own meat alternatives made using mycoprotein, such as sausages, burgers, steaks, mince, ham, and even bacon, so keep an eye out for a slightly cheaper alternative if you're not sure you'll like the taste.

Linda McCartney

Linda McCartney products such as Vegemince, are similar to Quorn, made using textured soya protein and wheat and generally bought frozen. As it's precooked with flavouring and absorbs liquids easily it works well in chilli, Bolognese, stews and curries. The texture is similar to meat mince so makes a good alternative to meat and many meat-eaters won't even notice they are eating soya protein when disguised in a shepherd's pie or lasagne!

Linda McCartney products include:

- sausages
- mince
- ready meals such as lasagne and cottage pie.

For more information and recipe ideas using Linda McCartney products, visit www.lindamccartneyfoods.co.uk.

Textured vegetable protein

Textured vegetable protein (TVP), sometimes called soya mince, is another type of meat alternative. Generally bought as a dry product it is available in mince, chunks or flakes, and needs liquid and flavour added to it as it doesn't taste of much on its own. The good news is that TVP absorbs liquid and flavouring superbly and when hydrated has a good texture that again works well in chilli, Bolognese and stew dishes. Another bonus of TVP is that as it's dry, it can be stored in your food cupboard for a decent amount of time and is less expensive to buy than fresh soya products, while providing a similar amount of protein.

Granose Soya Mince is readily available in most UK supermarkets and is a great vegetarian substitute for high-fat beef mince. It is well worth cooking for non-vegetarians as well!

CONVENIENCE/READY-MADE FOODS

While it is great to aspire to cooking every meal you eat from scratch using plenty of fresh ingredients, there are times, after a long day at work or a busy week, that a quick fix ready meal is in order. The good news is that the vegetarian ready meal market is growing fast, and while not recommended every day these meals do provide a solution when your belly is grumbling and your cupboard is bare.

Nowadays, it is possible to buy vegetarian cottage pie, lasagne, pasta, curry, Thai and even sushi dishes from brands such as Quorn, Cauldron and supermarket own brands. Additionally, there are also companies that specialise in providing a door-to-door service of home-cooked frozen vegetarian ready meals, so there is no excuse to eat poorly just because you are busy (see the section on delivery schemes later in the chapter).

MILK AND DAIRY ALTERNATIVES

There is a good range of milk and dairy alternatives for vegetarians who follow a vegan or ovo-vegetarian diet or need to avoid milk and dairy because of a dairy allergy or lactose intolerance.

SOYA MILK

Made from soya bean curd, soya milk is the most widely available dairy-free milk alternative. It can be bought in all major supermarkets, health food stores and increasingly in smaller shops. Reasonably priced, it is the most cost-effective milk alternative.

Soya milk comes sweetened or unsweetened and makes a great milk alternative in cooking, baking, or simply poured on your cornflakes in the morning. It does have a distinctive taste and is thicker than cow's milk, but if you want to avoid dairy it's a great choice.

Alpro is the biggest brand of soya milk and can be bought in most supermarkets. They produce not only regular flavoured soya milk, but also chocolate, vanilla, orange and vitamin-enriched varieties.

NUT MILK

After soya milk, almond or hazelnut milk is the next most common dairy-free alternative. Like soya milk, almond and hazelnut milks are high in protein and good fats and vitamin E.

While almond milk has a unique taste that may take a little getting used to, the milk itself blends well when used in cooking, added to milkshakes or in hot drinks. On the downside, if you have nut intolerance, you will need to find another alternative.

Nut milk can be a little harder to come by, though the main brand is Ecomil. You can order nut milk from www.goodness-direct.co.uk.

Pocket tip ❧

Soya and almond milks can be quite allergenic for some people. For those concerned about feeding young children, sticking to dairy milk or choosing a rice- or oat-based milk might be a safer option until they are older and you can be sure to avoid an allergic reaction.

RICE MILK

Rice milk can be quite sweet and is often sold with a light vanilla flavour. It is a rather watery milk alternative so is not great to use in cooking certain dishes that require a creamy and thicker milk. It is also low in protein, compared to other types of milk so does not make a nutritious milk replacement unless it has been fortified with vitamins and protein, which some brands are. However, it does work well as a drink and on cereal. Rice Dream is the most popular variety and can be bought in Sainsbury's and other supermarkets.

COCONUT MILK

Nutritionally coconut milk is low in protein. However, the sweet-tasting milk works well in cooking dairy-free creamy curry dishes or desserts. While the milk is low in calories it is quite high in saturated fat. Coconut milk can be bought in cartons, in cans or even in dried blocks and shredded straight into dishes when cooking where it will dissolve. Blue Dragon, one of the UK's biggest

Chinese food manufacturers, has coconut milk widely available in supermarkets. Likewise, some stores have own brand which is just as good.

HEMP MILK

One of the more recent milk alternatives to hit the market is hemp milk. It is made using soaked and drained hemp seeds which are blended and then water is strained through the seeds to form the milk. It has more protein than rice milk but less than soya milk and is quite watery when poured. It does work well in cooking though and in hot drinks and of course on those all-important cornflakes.

As it is less common it can be tricky to find and is best found in a specialist health food store or ordered online from www.good-nessdirect.com or www.ocado.com. The best brand is incredibly called Good Hemp Milk and they also produce other vegetarian products. Their full range can be found on their website www.goodwebsite.co.uk.

OAT MILK

Oat milk has a moderate amount of protein making it a better option than rice milk for cooking and topping up your protein levels. Oat milk has a mild and slightly nutty taste and works particularly well in a steaming hot bowl of porridge on a cold winter morning. Oatly is the biggest brand and is readily available in most major supermarkets.

Pocket tip ⚜

Oat milk may not be suitable for people with coeliac disease who are sensitive to the avenin protein present in oats. They should try soya milk or a nut milk such as almond.

VEGETARIAN CHEESE

Not all cheeses are vegetarian friendly as some are commonly made using rennet, an enzyme derived from the stomach of slaughtered animals. However, greater awareness of vegetarian products has led to a larger selection of vegetarian cheeses that are made using a plant enzyme instead. Most cheeses are labelled as to whether they are suitable for vegetarians.

Redwood produce a variety of different cheeses which are suitable for vegetarians: blue cheese, red cheddar, pepper jack and more. They are widely available in UK supermarkets and their range can be found online at www.redwoodfoods.co.uk.

 VEGETARIAN WINE AND BEER

Many wines, beers and spirits use animal products in the 'refining' production stages or as an ingredient. Gelatine, made from the connective bones and tissues of animals, is commonly used.

It would be impossible to list all of the different brands in this book, although you can search online for specific information. Veggie Wines (www.veggiewines.co.uk) has a near exhaustive list of the vegetarian status of wines, beers and spirits commonly sold in UK supermarkets.

You can also order a variety of vegetarian and vegan wines from Vintage Roots, which has an online shop, www.vintageroots.co.uk.

TIPS FOR THE PUB

Here are a few commonly found drinks in the pub which are reported as vegetarian.

Lagers	Beers	Cider	Spirits
Becks	Leffe	Westons	Absolut/Smirnoff Vodka
Heineken	Duvel	Magners Pear	Gordon's/Tanqueray Gin
Stella Artois	Chimay	Scrumpy Jack	Jack Daniels

Wines are far more difficult to list as there are so many, yet in a standard high street pub you may well come across brands such as Hardys, Jacob's Creek or Gallo. These are all suitable for vegetarians, although not for vegans.

VEGETARIAN STORE CUPBOARD INGREDIENTS

This is just a rough guide of what a vegetarian food cupboard should contain and it is likely that you will already have many of the goods suggested. As you become more familiar with cooking vegetarian food you will know what you need when you go shopping, and will soon find that your store cupboard has everything you need to create a fantastic meal.

LONG TERM STORAGE

The following can be found in most major supermarkets and health food stores.

Cooking oils and seasonings

The most commonly used cooking oils are vegetarian and vegan friendly, but many less common oils can be extremely beneficial for health, such as rapeseed oil, flaxseed oil and hemp oil as they are higher in the good fats that vegetarians need.

- olive oil (extra virgin or normal)
- sunflower oil
- vegetable oil
- rapeseed oil
- canola oil
- non-stick vegetable or olive spray

Condiments

- golden syrup
- honey

- fruit jams
- marmalade
- tomato paste
- white and red wine vinegar
- ketchup
- mayonnaise

Basic seasonings

- dried herbs such as basil, mixed herbs, sage, rosemary, thyme, etc
- rock salt
- pepper
- vegetarian bouillon
- chilli powder
- curry powder
- paprika
- tabasco
- soy sauce

Pocket tip ⚜

Try using a spray oil to coat a pan or food to avoid using too much oil. A decent non-stick pan or wok for stir frying will also enable you to use less oil and help keep calories down.

Tinned goods

- tomatoes: whole or chopped can be used to form the basis of a tomato sauce or soup
- vegetables: sweetcorn, peas, carrots, etc

- pulses: chickpeas, kidney beans, haricot beans, black beans, etc. While these are more expensive than the dried variety they are useful to have in as they can be used straight away rather than soaking overnight

- soups: vegetable, tomato, lentil, etc

- baked beans: always useful to have

Dried grains

- brown and white rice

- wild rice

- bulgur wheat

- couscous

- quinoa

- wholegrain and white pasta: spaghetti, penne, farfelle, lasagne sheets, etc

- porridge oats

- muesli

- wholegrain cereals

Dried beans and pulses

- chickpeas

- red and green lentils

- red kidney beans

- black-eyed beans

Nuts and seeds

- pumpkin, sesame, flax seeds

- unsalted nuts such as brazil nuts, almonds, pine nuts, hazel nuts, walnuts, pecan nuts, peanuts, etc

- peanut butter with no added sugar

Thickeners

- tahini (sesame paste)
- agar-agar
- cornstarch

Pocket tip ⚜

Luckily, the vast majority of foods sold by major retailers today contain a 'V' symbol to specify when it is suitable for vegetarians. If you are following a vegan diet or a non-lacto or ovo-vegetarian diet you will need to check the ingredients more carefully as many vegetarian products contain dairy and egg.

Frozen goods

- frozen vegetables such as mixed vegetables, peas, sweetcorn, spinach, etc
- frozen berries
- frozen vegetarian sausages, mince, and cutlets.

Frozen goods

Frozen vegetables and fruit are in fact highly nutritious and are comparable with fresh produce in terms of their nutritional value – provided they are frozen immediately after harvesting. In fact, studies by the European Food Information Council suggest that frozen food, if frozen correctly, can contain more nutrients than fresh produce. This is because fresh fruit and vegetables lose nutrients at a rate of approximately 10%–15% when stored at room temperature.

Invented by Clarence Birdseye in the early 20th century, blast, or flash freezing, is the process used by food manufacturers to freeze perishable goods quickly. Using liquid nitrogen the produce is subjected to cryogenic temperatures to ensure none of the nutritional goodness is lost and the quality is retained when cooked.

If you want to eat vegetables and fruits out of season, but don't want to spend a fortune, buying frozen produce is an easy way to do this.

SHORTER SHELF-LIFE INGREDIENTS

The following are fresh ingredients which make good additions to your weekly shopping list to help you create varied and exciting vegetarian dishes.

Eggs and dairy produce

- free-range or organic eggs: alternatively you can use an egg substitute if you prefer not to eat eggs

- cheese: either full-fat or reduced fat depending on preference such as mature cheddar, goat's cheese, feta, mozzarella, cream cheese; soya alternatives can be bought if you don't eat dairy

- low-fat yogurt: Greek or natural; again soya yogurts can easily be used to replace dairy types

- milk: cow, goat's (either full-fat, semi-skimmed or skimmed) or soya

- butter: unsalted or salted

- low-fat spread

(See p.176 for vegan alternatives.)

Fresh produce

- fruit such as apples, bananas, oranges, kiwi, lemons

- vegetables such as carrots, runner beans, mushrooms, broccoli, peppers

- salad goods such as lettuce, tomatoes, cucumber, radishes

- onions
- garlic

Other

- tofu
- vegetarian sausages
- vegetarian steak, bacon, and chicken-style pieces

VEGETARIAN-FRIENDLY DRINKS

Being a vegetarian doesn't mean you have to give up your morning cuppa. The following are all vegetarian-friendly drinks:

- tea and coffee – either caffeinated or decaffeinated
- herbal teas
- green tea
- fruit juice
- squash
- vegetarian wine and beer.

ETHICAL FOOD SHOPPING

Having tempted you with all these vegetarian treats, it would be somewhat unfair not to give you some advice on where to come by them. Although the high street and supermarkets are becoming increasingly veggie friendly, at times it can be difficult to find everything you need for an exciting vegetarian diet in the one place. The growth of online shopping, however, has meant that this is no longer a problem. This section aims to direct you to valuable online resources which can help you fill the gaps in your shopping basket easily.

ONLINE SHOPPING

Many people are abandoning the high street because of the bargains to be had online and the convenience of having shopping brought to your front door. Vegetarians are no different and there has been an enormous growth in the availability of specialist vegetarian retailers online.

Top vegetarian shops online

- **Goodness Direct** sells a good range of vegetarian, vegan and ethical and organic products. Visit www.goodnessdirect.co.uk.

- **Veggie Stuff** is a vegetarian and vegan food shop with a wide variety of products that you might not find in your local supermarket. A good choice for those vegetarians who live a little further away from the nearest big shops. Visit www.veggie-stuff.com.

- **Honest to Goodness** is a vegan store selling products for your store cupboard and dietary supplements – www.honest-to-goodness.org.uk.

- **Ethical Superstore** is a one stop shop for foods and clothes shopping. Visit www.ethicalsuperstore.com.

- **Alternative Stores** has a huge list of clothing, cosmetics and some foodstuffs available. Visit www.alternativestores.com.

- **Big Green Smile** sells a variety of eco-friendly products made using natural ingredients. They are UK based and good for cosmetics amongst other things. Visit www.biggreensmile.com.

DELIVERY SCHEMES

Locally produced or seasonal fruit and vegetables can be bought and delivered from a range of companies in the UK. Many companies also offer ready-made healthy vegetarian fare when you want a home cooked meal but are pressed for time.

- **Earth Natural Foods** delivers organic fruit and vegetables, ready meals, tea, coffee, organic chocolate and so on across London, Oxford and Greater London. Every bag contains a seasonal selection of organic produce and is priced between £9.50 and £19.95 a box. Visit www.earthnaturalfoods.co.uk.

- **Riverford Organic** delivers organic vegetable boxes to homes and restaurants across the South West of England and offers a lovely, earthy selection of local and seasonal produce. Visit www.riverford.co.uk.

- **Wild Carrot** in Buxton, Derbyshire specialises in organic food boxes, alcohol and environmentally-friendly products, and delivers to Buxton and surrounding areas. Expect to pay from £10 a box. Visit www.wildcarrot.freeserve.co.uk.

- **Organics To Go** sells and delivers fresh and seasonal fruit and vegetables, eggs, and Welsh cheeses to Wales, the West, Wiltshire and London. Visit www.organicstogo.co.uk.

- **The wholeshebag** delivers organic fruit and vegetable boxes in Scotland. Visit www.thewholeshebag.com.

For vegetarian ready meal deliveries try:

- **Lady of Shallott**, based in Sheffield, offers an appetising range of vegetarian ready meals. Visit www.ladyofshallott.co.uk.

- **Wiltshire Farm Foods** has outlets across the UK and can deliver a good range of vegetarian meals. Visit www.wiltshirefarmfoods.com.

Pocket tip ⚓

If you're feeling adventurous, try giving raw vegetarian cuisine a go. The raw diet has gained popularity among many celebrities. The company Raw Fairies deliver innovative gourmet raw vegetarian dishes to the London area. Visit www.rawfairies.com.

READING LABELS

Reading food labels can help you make a more informed choice about what you are eating. For example, if you are looking to reduce your intake of saturated fats and salt you can easily check the label and choose a lower-fat option.

Most products sold in supermarkets, health food stores and even in restaurants are now marked with a 'V' symbol to show it is suitable for vegetarians and 'VG' for vegans. Most supermarkets in the UK now also have dedicated vegetarian sections in the store which include fresh produce and frozen goods.

Changes to food labelling

The Food Standards Agency (FSA) first provided official guidance on labelling produce for vegetarians and vegans in 2006. This guidance also gave vegetarians the right to make an official complaint to Trading Standards against a food manufacturer which has mislabelled its produce as vegetarian when in fact it contains some ingredients that aren't suitable for vegetarians, or if evidence suggests that the food was in some way contaminated by an animal product.

Labels such as 'suitable for vegetarians' and 'suitable for vegans' fall under the Trade Descriptions Act 1968, which prohibits false or misleading labelling.

In 2010 the FSA guidance was also adopted in principle by the European Parliament.

While this all signifies progress for vegetarians at present, it is still voluntary for manufacturers to label products as suitable for vegetarian or vegan, which is something the vegetarian and vegan societies are campaigning to change.

 VEGETARIAN PRODUCTS

Some people not only prefer to eat a vegetarian diet they also choose to use vegetarian products which are more in keeping with their ethical or moral values. Here is a selection of vegetarian-friendly products.

THE VEGETARIAN WARDROBE

Vegetarian outfits don't have to be Glastonbury cast-offs, nor do they have to be boring. Natural materials can be used to produce ethical and attractive garments with real appeal but without cruelty.

Jackets, belts and bags made without the need for animal by-products or animal testing are also widely available. Check out the following websites for a huge range which will suit men and women of all shapes and sizes:

- www.vegetarian-shoes.co.uk
- www.freerangers.co.uk
- www.bboheme.com
- www.fashion-conscience.com
- www.neoncollective.com
- www.herbivoreclothing.com.

Shoes

While the majority of shoes are made using leather, vegetarian shoes are free from animal products and are made using a synthetic micro-fibre material used for yachting upholstery. There are a great variety of vegetarian shoes available: from brogues to boat shoes and sandals to strappy numbers. It can be difficult to be sure that shoes are vegetarian when buying them on the high street and it is often wiser to order them from the internet. Most stores will allow you to return products if there are issues with sizing.

One of the most high profile vegetarian shoes produced recently was the Blackspot sneaker produced by the organisation Adbusters. The Blackspot was intended to combat the dominance of Nike in the marketplace with an ethical alternative. The materials used are sustainably sourced and produced as well as being suitable for vegetarians. Likewise, all the shoes are produced in unionised workshops with good working conditions. You can find more information and order from their website www.adbusters.org/campaigns/blackspot.

Pocket fact 🖋

Celebrity and vegetarian fashion is becoming increasingly popular with designers such as Stella McCartney, who are creating ethical and eco-friendly stylish designer clothes. What makes Stella's success so remarkable is that she has managed to design catwalk-worthy clothes without using animal products such as leather or fur.

VEGETARIAN CLEANING PRODUCTS

Not all cleaning products are vegetarian friendly as they either contain animal products or have been tested on animals. Some products will state on the label whether they contain animal products and that they have not been tested on animals.

Brands worth looking out for are:

- **Faith in Nature** have a range of cleaning products from dishwasher gel to washing up liquid.

- **E-cover** products are available in many supermarkets and are environmentally friendly and good for sensitive skin.

- **Bio-D** produces dishwasher powder in biodegradable paper bags to help reduce waste.

- **Eco-zone** produce washing aids called Eco-balls to try and make your washing machine more efficient. They also have a range of environmentally friendly cleaning powders and liquids.

The Vegetarian Society provides a comprehensive list that is useful and many companies sell only vegetarian- and vegan-friendly cleaning products. You can also look online at the stores mentioned in this chapter.

VEGGIE COSMETICS

Cosmetic products are often the products most readily associated with animal testing and exploitative production methods. Yet, it's possible to look good without cruelty.

It is perfectly possible to find good-smelling deodorants and hair products that don't impinge on your lifestyle choices.

- **Tom's of Maine** deodorants are a great option for vegetarians. Visit www.tomsofmaine.com.

- **The Jason Natural** range of products has everything from toothpaste to deodorant and shampoo. They can be difficult to get on the high street, so you may have to look online. Visit www.jason-natural.com.

- If you're looking for cosmetics online, then you can find a full range at **Honesty** cosmetics, which provides good information on the ingredients of all their products. Visit www.honestycosmetics.co.uk.

On the high street

The high street store Lush stocks a variety of vegetarian-friendly cosmetics made using natural ingredients. They are endorsed by the Vegetarian Society and have an ingredient list online that will allow you to know exactly what's in your pot of fizzing bath powders or face cream.

The Co-operative supermarket and Marks & Spencer are both committed to cutting out animal testing and are model retailers for their labelling of vegetarian-friendly cosmetics.

Boots can be a good place to find veggie-friendly cosmetics, though you have to be careful to check the label as Boots is not yet registered as having fully excluded animal tested products. The make-up brand Urban Decay has many vegetarian-friendly products which are available in Boots stores. Boots also stock products from Burt's Bees, an American company which uses all natural products such as beeswax and honey.

Superdrug is fully BUAV (The British Union for the Abolition of Vivisection) accredited and has a good range of cosmetics which are vegetarian friendly and cruelty-free. They clearly label products which are acceptable for vegetarians and those concerned with animal welfare. This can be a great option for finding affordable shampoos, deodorants and other lotions and potions.

Likewise, The Body Shop is an old favourite which shuns products tested on animals. Many of their products are vegetarian friendly and they are almost always happy to advise on what is suitable in store.

4

COOKING

Everybody has the ability to cook a vegetarian meal, however simple. Vegetarian cooking can allow you to be creative and experimental, and provides a great chance to try exciting new foods that you may not have used in cooking before. This doesn't need to mean hours slaving over a stove though, or resorting to an endless diet of lentils. This chapter will provide advice on vegetarian food, shopping, preparation, cooking techniques. Rest assured after a little practise, and yes perhaps a bit of trial and error (all part of the fun!), you will be rustling up vegetarian delights in no time.

🥕 HYGIENE 🥕

While vegetarian cooking doesn't carry the same risks as cooking meat in terms of food poisoning, germs lurk on door handles and work surfaces so it is still very important to practise good hygiene when cooking.

Try not to lick your fingers or cooking utensils when preparing food but it is fine to taste as you go along. Just rinse the spoon before you put it back in the dish. In fact it is recommended to taste to check that you have added enough seasoning and flavouring, rather than just hope for the best.

Tantalising the taste buds

Humans have around 10,000 tiny taste buds on the tongue and roof of the mouth which all detect subtle flavours in food by sending a sensory message to the brain. However, everyone's palate is different: while one person may love salty foods another may have a 'sweet tooth' and love all things sweet. As we age our taste buds become less sensitive which is why children often dislike foods with a distinctive or strong taste. This is one of the reasons there may be foods you disliked as a child but enjoy now.

If you want to look after your palate avoid smoking as it irritates your taste buds and often gradually ruins the sense of taste. Some medications and illness can also affect the taste buds. To cleanse your palate while cooking, try nibbling a slice or two of cucumber, or a spoon of natural yogurt. Avoid mints or chewing gum as this won't actually cleanse the palate – just give you a nice minty mouth!

 PEELING AND CHOPPING FRUIT AND VEGETABLES

You'll need a decent peeler, a sharp knife and a sturdy chopping board.

Here are some specific tips for vegetable preparation.

- Most green vegetables won't require peeling. A thorough wash in cold water should suffice to remove any soil, insects (not ideal for a vegetarian!) and dirt.

- When chopping broccoli you may wish to remove the bulk of the stalk, although some people like to eat that too.

- For runner beans, the tops and tails simply need trimming away, which can then be cut into slides or strips depending on the dish.

- Carrots are generally peeled, and the tops and tails removed. The carrot can then either be cut into round slices, sticks or even grated into salads.

Potatoes: one of your five a day?

Although, botanically potatoes are part of the vegetable family, nutritionally they are not considered one of your five a day as they are a carbohydrate and a starchy food. However, this is something the Fresh Potato Suppliers Association is campaigning to change. They are striving to have potatoes included in the government's healthy-eating scheme.

Does the potato industry have a point? Well, nutritionally a medium-sized potato with the skin on provides 27mg of vitamin C, which is 45% of the recommended daily amount (RDA) for an adult. It also contains 0.2mg of vitamin B6 – 10% of the RDA – and traces of vitamins B1, B2, and the minerals magnesium, zinc, niacin and phosphorous which are beneficial to good health.

However, in common cooked forms of potatoes, such as deep fried chips and very oily roast potatoes, the skin has been removed and they contain high levels of fat.

To get the most out of your potato try making potato skins, which are a healthier choice than chips. The skins of new potatoes are more delicate and shouldn't need peeling or chopping – just give them a wash and sling them in the pot. Potatoes generally require a good scrub with a brush under cold water to remove excess soil and a small knife to remove any stalks.

The humble spud comes in all shapes and sizes so just make sure you try a healthy cooking method to get the most out of them.

COOKING VEGETABLES

Cooking vegetables is easy, but remember that they can be easily overcooked, which can destroy some of the essential nutrients and vitamins so learning how to cook vegetables correctly is vital.

BOILING

This is an efficient way to cook vegetables such as carrots, broccoli, peas, sweetcorn and potatoes. All that is required is a medium- or large-sized saucepan, depending on the quantity of vegetables you are cooking.

Wash and peel, if necessary, and chop your vegetables into evenly sized pieces. It is always a good idea to keep portion size consistent so that the pieces cook evenly.

Fill the pan with cold water and bring to the boil. Alternatively you can boil the kettle and add boiling water straight into the pan. When the water has reached full boil and is bubbling add the vegetables.

Average cooking times

This is just a guide as you may prefer your veggies with more or less bite, and the cooking time does vary depending on the size of the vegetable:

- carrots: 10 minutes

- broccoli: 7–8 minutes

- fresh peas: 6 minutes

- fresh sweetcorn: 6 minutes

- frozen vegetables: 5 minutes

- potatoes: 15–20 minutes.

Pocket tip ❧

If you are going to be making gravy stock or a sauce add the water the vegetables were boiled in to the mix, as any nutrients leaked from the vegetables in the boiling process will be in the water.

STEAMING

Nutritionists and health experts argue that steam cooking is the healthiest way to cook vegetables, as the vegetables steam in the water vapour instead of the water itself, helping to preserve more nutrients.

> ### Pocket fact
>
> *Steam cooking is traditionally used in Asian cooking, in particular, in Chinese dishes such as dumplings, or to cook Japanese or Thai sticky rice.*

Like boiling, steaming is also an easy, quick and cheap way to cook vegetables and can be combined with boiling rice, pasta or potatoes. Place a collapsible stainless steel steamer or bamboo steamer over the top of the pan and use the steam to cook the vegetables – thus saving excess water and washing up. If you don't have a steam rack, a wire colander or sieve will work just as well.

Alternatively, a good range of more modern electric steamers are available with a timer included. If you plan to steam cook a lot it may be worth investing in this type of steamer, which can be found in all good high street homeware shops, specialist kitchen shops and many supermarkets.

The majority of vegetables steam well, the exception being potatoes, which require boiling, baking or roasting.

To steam vegetables lay them evenly along the base of the steamer and carefully place the steamer at the top of the pan of boiling water, taking care not to insert it into the water itself. Cover the pan with a lid and reduce the heat to low or medium so that the water is just gently bubbling. Take care not to let the pan run dry as this can damage your pan and cause it to overheat.

Average cooking times for steaming are similar to boiling times (see p.73).

MICROWAVING

If time is of the essence, microwaving is the way to go. Vegetables can be prepared in the same way as other cooking techniques and should be placed in a microwavable container. There is now a good range of microwavable containers made specifically for vegetables.

Pocket fact 🌶

Microwaving is as healthy as steaming in terms of preserving the nutrients found in vegetables.

Average cooking times are a couple of minutes less than with boiling and steaming; however, it depends on the voltage power of your microwave so be sure to check the product instructions first.

STIR FRYING

Stir frying is traditionally used in Asian cooking and involves high heat and short cooking times. A number of delicious vegetarian dishes can be made using this cooking method, so it is definitely worth mastering the art of stir frying.

To stir fry effectively use a wok or a good-quality non-stick pan. When stir frying vegetables, cut smaller pieces than you would for boiling or steaming to help them cook faster. Bean shoots, peppers, and green vegetables stir fry well and are used in most Asian dishes.

First add oil to the pan. This can be any oil you like, such as sunflower, vegetable, rapeseed, olive, nut or even linseed oil, it really depends on the dish you are cooking as the flavour of the oil can be used to enhance the dish. Next add onions, if you are using them, and any flavour enhancements (such as garlic, ginger and chilli, or herbs and spices). Fry until the onion begins to turn brown and then add either your tofu or mycoprotein, if you are cooking with them and fry until brown. Next add your vegetables and continue frying the ingredients while stirring at the same time until they have cooked. It is important to keep the heat turned up while stir frying – this may set off the smoke alarm, so turn on an extractor fan if you have one or open a window.

Pocket tip 🌱

Try steam frying as an alternative to traditional oil frying. To do this halve the amount of oil used in frying and add a little water or vegetable stock. Place a lid over the top of the pan for a few minutes to help steam the food.

GRILLING

Grilled vegetables or food are cooked using the direct heat from the oven grill, and grilling is a healthy way of cooking as any fat from the food drips into the grill tray below. When cooking using the grill you need to keep an eye on it and turn the item regularly as it will cook fairly quickly. For example, when grilling vegetarian sausages or burgers, cooking time from fresh is generally just 10 minutes and from frozen just add another 4–5 minutes.

Grilled or barbequed vegetables taste delicious as they acquire a slightly smoky taste. Portobello mushrooms, buffalo tomatoes and peppers are examples of vegetables that grill well. It is advisable to lightly coat them with oil before grilling so that they don't stick to the grill rack.

ROASTING

Roasted vegetables have a richer taste than other cooking methods, as they cook for longer and generally absorb the taste of the oil and seasoning they are cooked in. For the perfect roast potato heat the oil in a large baking tin first before adding potatoes to it, sprinkle with salt and pepper. Then roast in the oven until golden and crispy. Fresh herbs such as rosemary, sage and parsley also work well in roasting.

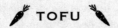 TOFU

Dread tofu no more and discover how to cook it to make the most of this simple ingredient. There are three main types of tofu sold in Western countries: silken, medium and firm.

Silken tofu

This is perfect for blending into sauces, scrambling as an egg alternative, covering dishes as a topping, mixing into salads, and even using as a dessert base. This kind of tofu generally comes in a cardboard box.

Pocket fact

In Japanese cuisine silken tofu comes in a block served as a salad, with soy sauce and grated ginger. It's a real test of your chopstick skills to pick up the tofu in one piece! Many Western tourists have tried and failed, to the amusement of the Japanese, who seem to have no trouble!

Medium tofu

This is a better choice for adding to chunkier salads, where the tofu is cut into chunks, adding to soups, and more solid desserts. This type of tofu often comes in a plastic box filled with water to keep it moist.

Firm and extra-firm tofu

This tofu has a more sturdy and rubbery texture when raw and is good for stir fry dishes, grilling as a steak or even roasting in the oven. This type of tofu also comes in a plastic box with water.

STORING TOFU

To store tofu after it has been opened it is best to place the remaining tofu in an air-tight plastic container filled with fresh water to keep the tofu fresh and moist. The tofu will keep like this for around three days, but it is advisable to change the water daily if you don't use it up the next day.

HOW TO COOK TOFU

First, you need to decide what kind of tofu will best suit the dish you are preparing. As a rule silken tofu is better used fresh or added to light Asian soups and curries and requires a lighter touch. Firmer tofu is better used in high heat cooking and you can be a bit heavier handed with this type.

Silken tofu

Silken tofu should be carefully drained and rinsed under cold water. Don't worry about drying the tofu too much as it doesn't matter if the tofu is still wet. Cut the portion size of tofu you want and carefully add to the top of salads, or place in a soup using a ladle. If you want to eat the tofu warm, allow it to simmer in the liquid for a couple of minutes and then serve.

To blend into a dressing or for a dessert use either a fork or a whisk and lightly beat the tofu into the desired consistency, and gently fold in flavouring and seasoning. Return to the fridge to chill for 30 minutes before serving.

Pocket tip ✤

To make tofu with a crispy or crunchy outer layer, take a regular block of tofu, wash and dry it carefully and cut into even chunks. Mix cornflour with water and a splash of oil and whatever seasoning you prefer — soy sauce works well — and soak the tofu in the mixture. Shallow fry until golden brown and crunchy.

Medium tofu

Medium tofu should be drained and rinsed in cold water before drying or draining using either kitchen paper or a clean tea towel. A good way to drain the tofu is to wrap the block in a tea towel and place it on a clean plate before carefully placing a weight on top for 10 minutes to allow the liquid to drain out.

To cook medium tofu with vegetables or noodles, cut the tofu into equal-sized chunks and add to the hot pan. This type of tofu is less likely to stay together but will create a lovely creamy texture to the dish. Stir over a low heat for five minutes and serve.

To serve chilled in a dessert, using a whisk blend the tofu and add the flavouring before spooning into ramekins or topping your cheesecake. Put in the fridge and allow to chill for one to two hours before serving.

Scrambling tofu

To scramble tofu, beat with a fork until smooth and add a pinch of salt and pepper and a drop of water. All types of tofu can be scrambled and which type you use just depends on the desired consistency of the end result.

Heat oil in a non-stick pan and add the tofu. Cook by stirring over a high heat until a golden brown colour. Onions, tomatoes and mushrooms can be added if desired. Serve on a slice of toast and enjoy!

Firm and extra firm tofu

Firm tofu should first be drained and rinsed in cold water. Next the tofu should be dried to remove all excess water using the same technique as the medium tofu. As this type of tofu is firmer greater weight can be added if necessary as the tofu is better at staying together.

If using for a stir fry dish first cut the tofu into equal-sized chunks around 1cm–2cm in length and width. Next heat a tablespoon of oil in a non-stick pan before adding the tofu and any flavouring. Gently fry until the tofu begins to turn brown and crisp before adding your other ingredients.

Firm tofu can be cut into 'steaks' and fried, grilled or baked. When grilling lightly coat the tofu with a dressing, miso paste (Japanese fermented soybean) works well and grill until it begins to turn brown.

Tempeh

Similar to tofu, tempeh is a more fermented soybean product commonly used in Indonesian cooking. It can be prepared using the same method as firm tofu and is great in stir fries and rice dishes. It can be bought at all good health food shops or online at www.freshtempeh.co.uk.

 **EATING SEASONALLY**

There are a number of good reasons to eat seasonal and local food, all of which are in keeping with what a wholesome vegetarian diet stands for. Eating seasonally can help reduce energy wastage associated with carbon dioxide emissions as food is not transported a long way from foreign countries.

Another reason people like to eat seasonally is that it helps them reconnect with the natural progression of the seasons and is a celebration of the passing of each new season. However, the most important reason we should all be eating seasonally, where possible, is the fact that seasonal food is fresher and tastes better.

Pocket tip ❧

Farmers' markets and local street markets are a good place to go to buy fresh seasonal produce – often at a cheaper price than larger retailers.

Most top chefs and restaurants like to use fresh, seasonal, local produce; however, even they think it is difficult to cook using 100% local produce as the choice is limited when you have an entire menu to fill. Where possible it makes sense to cook seasonally as it gives you an incentive to make the most of cooking creatively using a limited product or allows you to form your own meal traditions each year, but don't feel guilty if you don't only use seasonal ingredients.

Pocket tip ⚜

Create your own seasonal selection of recipes that you enjoy eating at certain times of the year, and you will find you always have something to look forward to, whether it's strawberries and cream in the summer or autumnal pumpkin soup.

UK SEASONAL FOOD CALENDAR

Make the most of what's in season by experimenting with some less common vegetables and fruit. Use this calendar to help you follow what food is available when and to inspire you to create some exciting seasonal dishes.

Pocket tip ⚜

Just because food is seasonal doesn't always mean it is sourced locally as it could have been grown in another part of the country. To buy local seasonal food, visit your nearest farmers' market or farm shop.

January and February

Purple sprouting broccoli is packed full of iron and can be added to curries, pasta or stir fry noodle dishes. Alternatively it can be served as a side dish with a drizzle of olive oil and a bit of salt and pepper.

Try this

Add purple sprouting broccoli to cauliflower cheese for a twist on the traditional recipe and to inject a little colour.

Also available

- peppers
- potatoes
- apples
- cabbages
- parsnips
- leeks.

March

Spinach is rich in vitamins and minerals, and is also full of health-promoting phytonutrients (substances found in some plants which are believed to be beneficial to human health) such as carotenoids including: beta-carotene, lutein, and zeaxanthin and flavonoids which are full of antioxidants.

Try this

Add baby spinach to salads or lightly steam larger varieties and add to a homemade pasta sauce.

Also available

- lettuce
- spring greens
- watercress
- new potatoes.

Pocket tip ⚜

Try to buy fruit and vegetables in season to limit your exposure to chemicals used to prolong shelf life and preserve colour. Buying in season also means that you will have a different selection of foods to choose from each month.

April

Asparagus is high in vitamins A, B and C, folate and potassium. It is thought to have anti-inflammatory benefits and to be good for the digestion.

Try this

Add lightly steamed asparagus to pasta dishes, or to scrambled egg or tofu for a healthy lunch.

Also available

- apricots
- lamb's lettuce
- peas
- radishes
- gooseberries
- strawberries.

May

Artichoke is part of the thistle family and like the supplement milk thistle is excellent for detoxifying the liver, helping to protect against infection. Artichokes provide a good source of vitamins A and C, folic acid, magnesium, potassium, niacin, riboflavin and thiamine, all needed for good health. Artichokes work well added to pasta and rice dishes or eaten as a side dish.

Try this

Peel and halve an artichoke, removing the tough stalk. Take a large red pepper cut in half and pop the artichoke into the pepper. Season with salt, pepper and dried parsley. Drizzle with olive oil and roast in the oven for 30 minutes.

Also available

- aubergines
- fennel
- courgettes

- raspberries

- tomatoes

- watermelons.

June

Beetroot is an earthy root vegetable that has a number of health benefits, including helping to reduce high blood pressure and acting as a muscle anti-inflammatory. The bright colour of the beet is known as betacyanin, which is believed to have powerful antioxidant properties. Beets are also a good source of vitamins A and C, iron, calcium and folic acid. Can be eaten raw, grated or sliced into salads or cooked.

Try this

Top a flattened sheet of puff pastry with sliced beetroot, goat's cheese, chopped walnuts and fresh basil. Cook for 20 minutes at 180°C, or until golden brown, for a quick and healthy light meal.

Also available

- basil

- garlic

- blackcurrants

- redcurrants

- blueberries

- cherries

- peaches.

Pocket tip ❧

The Eat Seasonably website (www.eatseasonably.co.uk) tells you which fruits and vegetables are in season each month, and offers recipes and serving suggestions. You can also download a colourful calendar to put on the fridge.

July

Celeriac has a gnarly exterior but don't be put off as this root vegetable packs quite a punch as it is high in potassium, magnesium and the vitamin B6. It has a slightly nutty flavour and can be eaten on its own raw, or added to curries and stir fries.

Try this

Roughly slice half a celeriac, one red onion, half a red cabbage and grate three large carrots. Mix together with a tablespoon of red and white wine vinegar, a tablespoon of wholegrain mustard and a good pinch of salt and pepper to make a vegan-friendly coleslaw.

Also available

- broccoli
- sweetcorn
- figs
- plums.

August

Blackberries come into season at the end of the summer and the start of autumn and can either be bought from the supermarket or picked from wild hedgerows and bushes for free – which is far more fun and rewarding! Packed full of antioxidants and vitamins, blackberries can be frozen and used in pies and crumbles, to make jam or just eaten on their own.

Try this

Use one cup of fresh blackberries and two large cooking apples to make a delicious fruit crumble. Top with a crumble topping and bake for 35 minutes. Serve with custard or ice cream.

Pocket fact

The ancient Greeks used blackberries as a treatment for gout because of their anti-inflammatory properties.

Also available

- kale

- leeks

- damsons

- pears.

September

Unlike other types of tuber potatoes, sweet potatoes are root veg-etables and come in a range of white, orange and purple varieties. While providing an excellent source of vitamins, iron and folic acid, they also offer a good dose of dietary fibre essential for good bowel health. Sweet potatoes are delicious, baked, mashed, fried, and boiled, and work well in curries and soups.

Try this

As an alternative to traditional chips, cut a washed sweet potato into evenly sized wedges. Pop on a baking tray and lightly coat with oil – any type is fine – and sprinkle with paprika or mild chilli powder, salt and pepper. Oven cook at 200°C until crispy.

Also available

- pumpkins

- swedes

- turnips

- apples

- cranberries.

October

Dates are a powerful little fruit packed full of dietary fibre. They are perhaps best known for their laxative properties which help maintain a healthy colon, but they are also full of iron, potassium, and vitamins. The dark colour of the date is known as tannin, which is known to have anti-inflammatory and antiox-idant effects.

Try this

Add a handful of dried chopped dates to your morning porridge for a healthy breakfast fix.

Also available

- Jerusalem artichokes
- sweetcorn
- Cox apples.

November

Red cabbage is rich in vitamin C and antioxidants and is thought to help in stomach conditions such as an ulcer due to its anti-inflammatory properties.

Try this

Finely slice half a red cabbage, add one grated carrot, half a sliced white onion, two sliced apples, a handful of raisins, 1 tablespoon of red wine vinegar, olive oil and dill pickle, and mix together for a crunchy winter salad.

Also available

- cauliflowers
- potatoes.

December

Lemon is widely known for its medicinal health benefits, and useful for soothing a sore throat. They are also full of vitamin C and citric acid, which is useful for maintaining healthy kidney function. Lemons can be used in cooking, in drinks or as a part of healthy salad dressing.

Try this

Juice three large lemons and mix with cream cheese and icing sugar to make a simple cheesecake mix. Top onto a biscuit base and pop in the fridge for two hours.

Also available

- chicory
- white cabbages
- Brussels sprouts
- chards.

Pocket tip ⚜

You don't need much space to grow your own vegetables, fruits and herbs — just a corner of a garden will do, or you can even grow fresh herbs in a window box. The Allotment Pocket Bible has more in-depth advice about starting to grow your own food, or visit The National Vegetable Society website www.nvsuk.org.uk.

STORING FRUIT AND VEGETABLES

How you store your fruit, vegetables and fresh produce has a major effect on how long they last and how good they taste. While storing vegetarian food has less of the health hazards of storing meat, it is still important that good hygiene and care is taken.

FRUIT

Most fruit can be stored in a fridge, which will prolong its life. However, most don't need to be and can be stored in a cool, dry place in a fruit bowl.

Store bananas separately as they cause other fruits to ripen and go off more quickly. A banana tree hanger is the best place to store bananas and can be bought from most high street kitchen shops and many supermarkets.

Pocket tip ♣

If you want to hurry up the ripening time then pop a very ripe banana into the fruit bowl, with the other fruit, overnight.

Tomatoes are officially regarded as fruits and don't need to be stored in a fridge, although it is fine to do so if you prefer. Storing quickly perishable fruits such as strawberries, blueberries and grapes in a fridge is a good idea.

If you have an excess of fruit or vegetables just pop it in the freezer for a later use to save on waste. Bread and cakes containing fruit can also be frozen quite safely.

Pocket tip ♣

Cooking and freezing in batches is a great idea. Soups, stews, curries, and sauces can all be frozen for a later date. As a rule, use within one month.

VEGETABLES

Root vegetables, potatoes, onions and garlic don't need to be stored in a fridge. Store in a cool dark place – a cardboard box is fine. Vegetables such as broccoli, peppers, mushrooms, spinach and corn are best stored in a fridge.

Use-by dates

Although food manufacturers print use-by dates on all produce there has been some debate recently about this as the produce, in most cases, is perfectly safe for human consumption several days after the date has expired. Use your common sense – if the food looks and smells all right then it is likely to be fine to eat!

5

RECIPES

At first it may seem that it is more work to cook healthy and nutritious vegetarian food. But as you become accustomed to cooking vegetarian dishes you will find that it can be as easy and fun as cooking any other type of dish. Vegetarian cooking may involve expanding your culinary skills, which may be useful in the long term.

Now that you have crammed your store cupboard full of the basics and eradicated any lurking meat product offenders, it is time for the fun part – cooking! This chapter offers a selection of easy, healthy, and occasionally naughty, recipes for breakfast, lunch and dinner with a couple of simple snack ideas to keep you going in between. (For vegan recipes see pp.170–175.)

🥕 BREAKFAST 🥕

While all meals are important it is true that breakfast is the most important meal of the day. Eating a healthy and nutritious breakfast helps set you up for the day as it literally 'breaks the fast' on waking and helps boost concentration and keeps you more alert. If you eat breakfast you are also less likely to be tempted to raid the biscuit tin at 10am.

Porridge

Eaten regularly, oats can help reduce cholesterol, lower blood pressure and can aid weight loss. This is because oats are a wholegrain, slow-release food, meaning they help stabilise blood sugar levels and keep you feeling fuller for longer.

Porridge has regained popularity over the last couple of years. It can help weight loss and is also extremely cheap so it's perfect if you're trying to stick to a budget.

These well-balanced and simple breakfast recipes should help keep you going to lunch.

CRUNCHY FRUIT AND NUT MUESLI

Makes 8–10 portions

Ingredients

- 1kg jumbo rolled porridge oats
- 50g chopped brazil nuts
- 50g hazelnuts
- 50g almonds
- 75g mixed seeds (pumpkin, flaxseed, sunflower, etc.)
- 50g dried cranberries
- 50g dried chopped apricots
- 50g raisins

Method

1. Preheat the oven to 170°C.

2. Place the oats, nuts and seeds on a large baking tray and toast in the oven for 10 minutes, shaking and turning in the tray halfway through. Take the tray from the oven and leave to cool: this should take only about 10 minutes.

3. Mix the toasted ingredients well with the dried fruit.

4. Serve with cold milk or yogurt.

SUMMER FRUIT SOYA MILK PORRIDGE

Serves 1

Ingredients

- 50g jumbo porridge oats
- 250ml soya milk – more or less can be added depending on how thick or thin you prefer your porridge
- 1 banana, sliced
- Handful of fresh blueberries
- 5 fresh strawberries, sliced
- Runny honey to serve

Method

1. Put the oats and fruit in a saucepan and add the milk, bring to the boil and then immediately reduce the heat and allow to simmer, stirring continuously for approximately 5 minutes. If the porridge is too thick or thin at this stage for your taste you can either add more milk to thin it or cook for an extra 2 minutes to allow it to thicken.

2. Serve immediately, drizzled with honey.

Alternative suggestions

- If you don't want to use soya milk, cow's, goat's or nut milk can be used instead.
- Dried fruit such as raisins, apricots and cranberries can also be used to replace the fresh fruit.
- Try adding a sprinkle of brown sugar on the top or if you prefer a savoury taste try adding some salt.

BUCKWHEAT PANCAKES WITH BAKED PEACHES AND YOGURT

Serves 4

Ingredients

- 4 medium-sized peaches, de-stoned and cut into quarters
- Honey, to drizzle (or sugar)
- 150g buckwheat flour
- 90g self-raising flour
- 2tsp cinnamon
- 1tsp bicarbonate of soda
- 3 medium-sized eggs beaten
- 2tbsp caster sugar
- 284ml pot of buttermilk
- 1tbsp unsalted butter

Method

For the peaches:

1. Pre-heat the oven to 180°C. Place the peaches on a baking tray and drizzle with honey, or sprinkle with sugar. Bake until the peaches begin to caramelise and turn golden brown. Remove and set aside.

For the pancakes:

1. Whisk together the flour, sugar, cinnamon and bicarbonate of soda in a bowl. Form a well in the centre and fold in the beaten eggs. Gradually stir in the buttermilk and whisk until the batter is smooth.

2. Using a non-stick frying pan melt a little of the butter and coat the pan. Add a soup ladle of batter per pancake, and try to avoid spreading too thinly as the pancake should be thick and springy. Cook for a couple of minutes on each side until the

pancake starts to turn a golden brown. Remove from the pan and place on a warm plate under the grill to keep warm.

3. Cook the remaining batter until you have a stack of pancakes, allowing 2 or 3 per person.

Place the pancakes on a plate and top with the peach quarters and a dollop of Greek yogurt.

Alternative suggestions

- Other fruits also work well with this dish, either fresh or cooked. Try blueberries, strawberries or baked apples.

- You can also add just a drizzle of maple syrup and tuck in!

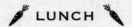 LUNCH

An easy vegetarian lunch doesn't have to consist of a boring cheese and pickle sandwich and a packet of crisps, which also isn't very healthy.

If you're short of time, but are tired of eating the same lunch each day, these simple recipes should give you a few ideas to try something different.

FALAFEL WITH GREEN SALAD AND PITTA

Serves 4

Ingredients

- 400g can chickpeas, rinsed and drained

- 2tbsp plain flour – you can use wholemeal flour here if you prefer or mix half and half

- 1 red onion, finely diced

- 2 cloves garlic, finely chopped

- 1 small mild green chilli deseeded and finely chopped – if you are preparing for children or adults that dislike spicy foods it is fine to leave the chilli out

- Sunflower or vegetable oil for frying
- Handful of flat-leaf parsley, roughly chopped – it is fine to use 2tsp dried herbs if you haven't got fresh to hand
- Handful of coriander, roughly chopped
- 1tsp cumin
- Splash of lemon juice
- Pinch of salt

Method

1. Rinse the chickpeas in cold water and roughly dry with kitchen paper or a tea towel.

2. Mix the chickpeas with the flour, onion, garlic, parsley, coriander, spices, chilli, salt and lemon juice. You may need to add a splash of oil if the mixture seems a little dry. Blend in a food processor until the mixture is smooth and has a little bounce to it.

3. Shape into 12 small patties or 4 large burger shapes.

4. Heat the oil in a non-stick frying pan, and add the burgers. The smaller patties will take less time to cook but on average cook for 3 minutes on each side until the falafels look lightly golden.

5. When cooked transfer to a plate and dab lightly with a piece of kitchen towel to remove excess oil.

Serve with green salad, hummus and salsa in a wholemeal toasted pitta bread.

Pocket tip 🌱

Homemade hummus is incredibly easy to make: take one 400g tin of chickpeas, drained and rinsed, the juice and rind of a lemon, two cloves of garlic (chopped), a tablespoon of tahini (sesame paste) and olive oil, salt and pepper. Blitz in a food processor and it's done.

ROASTED RED PEPPERS, SUN-DRIED TOMATOES AND HUMMUS TOASTED WRAPS

Serves 2

Ingredients

- 2 large red peppers, deseeded and cut into slices
- 2 whole cloves of garlic
- Olive oil for drizzling
- Pinch of salt and pepper
- 5 large sun-dried tomatoes, roughly sliced
- 2 wraps – white, brown or seeded
- Handful of fresh basil
- 1tbsp hummus per wrap

Method

1. Pre-heat the oven to 180°C.

2. Place the peppers and garlic on a baking tray and drizzle with olive oil, season and cook for 15 minutes or until the peppers are soft and beginning to brown.

3. Spread the hummus evenly on each wrap and top with the peppers and sun-dried tomatoes. Scatter the fresh basil on top. Roll and tuck the ends in to stop the filling falling out.

4. Using a griddle pan lightly toast the outside of the wrap to get a slightly smoky flavour, or pop back into the oven for 5 minutes.

Serve with a few vegetable crisps or salad.

Packed lunch

A great way to ensure you always have a healthy and nutritious lunch each day at work is to cook evening meals in larger batches than you need, so that you can take leftovers for lunch the next day. Never again will you need to turn to a soggy mayonnaise-filled sandwich when hunger hits. Taking lunch each day can save you money, in fact, buying lunch each day could equate to a whopping £1,000 a year!

CARROT AND CORIANDER SOUP WITH WHOLEMEAL ROLLS

Serves 2/4

Ingredients

- 500g carrots, roughly chopped

- 1 large white onion, finely sliced

- 2 cloves garlic, crushed

- 1tbsp oil

- 1tsp ground coriander

- 1 litre vegetable stock – use the boiled water the carrots were cooked in to make the most of the nutrients

- Bunch of fresh coriander, roughly chopped or torn

- 1tbsp single cream – use if you prefer a creamier soup

- Pinch of grated nutmeg

- Salt and pepper

Method

1. Peel and chop the carrots, and boil until cooked. In a large pan fry off the onion and garlic until the onions turn brown.

2. Using the boiling water from the carrots, mix up 1 litre of vegetable stock.

3. In a food processor blend the carrots, onions, garlic and add the nutmeg, salt and pepper and fresh coriander. Gradually add the stock and blend again until the soup has reached the preferred consistency.

4. Transfer to a large saucepan and warm the soup. Stir in the cream and serve immediately with a warmed roll.

Alternatives

Most vegetables make excellent soups. Good alternatives to carrot and coriander include leek and potato and broccoli and stilton. However, if you have a fridge full of vegetables that need eating up, creating a mixed vegetable soup using a hotchpotch of veggies works excellently and saves waste. Follow the same technique as the carrot recipe or roast the veggies first, blend, season, add stock and serve.

 **DINNER**

Nothing beats a home-cooked meal in the evening. Whether you are eating alone, or as a family, sitting down to an evening meal should be relaxing and is a good chance to catch-up on the day's events. These easy recipes don't take long to make and taste great.

CHICKPEA, SPINACH AND MUSHROOM COCONUT CURRY

Serves 4

Ingredients

- 1tbsp sunflower or vegetable oil
- 1 large red onion, chopped
- 2/3 cloves garlic, finely chopped
- 1tsp curry powder
- 1tsp cumin powder
- 1tsp cayenne pepper

- 1 red chilli
- 1 red pepper, deseeded and sliced
- 100g of button mushrooms, brushed and sliced
- 2 × 400g cans of chickpeas drained and rinsed – butterbeans or green lentils make a great alternative
- 5 large tomatoes, cut into quarters
- 1 bag of spinach, washed
- 1 can of coconut milk
- Salt and pepper
- 60g brown rice per person
- 2 large garlic and coriander naan breads (optional)

Pocket tip ⚜

For a less fiery curry, deseed the chilli, taking care to remove the seed membrane as this is where the heat of the chilli comes from. Wash your hands well and avoid rubbing your eyes! The coconut milk will also help cool the curry – add extra coconut milk or a spoonful of natural yogurt to cool the dish further.

Method

1. Heat the oil in a large non-stick pan, add the onion, garlic, spices and seasonings. Cook over a high heat until the onion is soft and golden.

2. Add the sliced red pepper and mushrooms and reduce the heat and slightly stir fry. Add the chickpeas, tomatoes and half the spinach.

3. Pour the coconut milk into the pan and allow to simmer on a low heat for 15 minutes. Add the remaining spinach and gently stir. Continue cooking for a further 20 minutes. If the curry requires liquid add a little water.

Serve with rice or naan bread.

Pocket tip ❧

Slow cooking a curry makes the flavour more pungent. Ideally, cook the curry the day before as the flavours will marinate overnight. Curry also freezes well so try making extra to use for lunch.

BUTTERNUT SQUASH RISOTTO

This simple yet hearty dish is packed full of flavour and is satisfyingly filling, making it a perfect choice when cooking for non-vegetarians.

Serves 4

Ingredients

- 1 large butternut squash peeled, deseeded and cut into rough cubes
- Good handful of fresh sage, chopped (dried is fine if fresh is unavailable)
- 1 large white onion, finely diced
- 2/3 cloves garlic, chopped
- 200g risotto rice
- 4 medium-sized tomatoes, chopped
- 1 litre instant vegetable stock
- 1 glass white wine
- Olive oil for drizzling
- Black pepper
- Salt
- 130g grated vegetarian parmesan cheese

Method

1. Put the oven on to heat at 200°C. Peel and deseed the butternut squash and chop roughly into cubes. Place on an oven tray and drizzle with olive oil and season with a pinch of salt and pepper and chopped sage. Put in the oven and roast for around 15/20 minutes or until the squash is soft enough to mash.

2. For the risotto, heat a little olive oil in a large non-stick pan. Add the onion, garlic and a pinch of salt and pepper to the pan. Fry and gently stir until the onions are starting to brown. Add the chopped tomatoes to the pan and gently fry for another 2 minutes.

3. Remove the butternut from the oven and roughly mash. Set to one side.

4. Add the rice to the onions, garlic and tomatoes and add more oil if necessary. Stir until all the rice is coated. Add some of the vegetable stock – use a ladle if necessary. Tip the butternut mixture into the pan and stir into the rice.

5. Add the glass of white wine in two halves giving the rice chance to absorb the liquid. Gradually add the remaining wine and stock stirring regularly for around 20 minutes – the risotto may need slightly longer depending on how much bite you prefer your rice to have. Add a handful of grated parmesan to the risotto and stir in.

6. When the risotto is cooked remove from the heat and sprinkle the remaining parmesan on top, and cover with a clean, slightly damp tea towel for 3–4 minutes to allow the cheese to melt and create a creamy texture. Divide into four portions and serve immediately.

Alternatives

To create a creamier risotto stir in a dollop of either single cream or crème fraiche while cooking.

CHICKPEA, LENTIL AND COURGETTE GRATIN

This simple dish makes a good veggie alternative to a Sunday lunch. It can be served with whichever vegetables are in season.

Serves 4

Ingredients

For the gratin:

- 1 large Spanish onion, thinly sliced
- 3 cloves garlic, finely chopped
- 1 large red or green pepper cut into slices
- 2 large courgettes cut into cubes
- 1 400g can of chickpeas
- 1 400g packet of puy lentils
- 1 tin of chopped tomatoes – or 6 large fresh tomatoes, chopped
- 1 pint of vegetable stock
- 1tbsp olive or extra virgin olive oil
- Salt and pepper
- Bunch of flat-leaf parsley
- 6 sun-dried tomatoes or 1tbsp sun-dried tomato paste

For the topping:

- 500g Greek or plain natural yogurt
- 500g crème fraiche
- Good handful grated vegetarian parmesan (or cheddar if you prefer)
- Salt and pepper

Method

1. Pre-heat the oven to 200°C.

2. Heat the oil in a large non-stick pan and fry the onions and garlic until the onions begin to brown. Add the courgettes, peppers, chickpeas, lentils, tomatoes and parsley, leaving a lit-

tle for the topping, and gradually add the stock. Cook on low
heat for 15 minutes, stirring occasionally. Season well with salt
and pepper adding more if needed.

3. Transfer to a large, ovenproof casserole dish and set aside.

For the topping:

4. Mix together the yogurt, crème fraiche, cheese, and season
well with salt and pepper.

5. Pour the topping on the gratin and sprinkle on a handful of
grated cheese and the remaining parsley. Oven cook for 35
minutes or until the topping has turned a golden brown.

Serve with fresh seasonal vegetables and chunks of French bread.

DESSERTS

For those of you with a sweet tooth, you might want to treat yourself to one of these delicious and decadent desserts that can be
made in advance — perfect if you are having a dinner party.

LIME AND GINGER CHEESECAKE WITH GRATED CHILLI CHOCOLATE

Serves 6/8

Ingredients

- 1 pack of 200g ginger biscuits – if you're not keen on ginger,
then digestives or other plain biscuits work well

- 3oz unsalted butter, melted

- 2 tubs of 250g mascarpone – cream cheese, ricotta or even
silken tofu can be used as an alternative

- 4 limes – juice and zest

- 3oz icing sugar

- 50g dark chilli chocolate grated – plain milk or dark chocolate
is fine if you don't like chilli chocolate

Method

1. Pre-heat the oven to 180°C. Crush the biscuits by hand or using a food processor. A food processor will help achieve a finer crumb.

2. Mix the biscuits with the melted butter and press into an 8-inch cake tin. Bake in the oven at 180°C for 20 minutes.

3. Allow to cool before adding the cheesecake topping.

4. Using a hand whisk or fork mix the mascarpone, lime juice and zest and icing sugar. Spread this evenly on the biscuit base and sprinkle the grated chocolate on top.

5. Refrigerate for 2 hours before serving.

Alternatives

If you want to make dainty mini cheesecakes just divide the mixture between six small ramekins.

APPLE AND APRICOT NUT CRUMBLE

Serves 6

Ingredients

- 3 large cooking apples, peeled and sliced
- 6 fresh apricots, sliced
- 1tsp dried cinnamon
- 125g brown sugar
- 100g plain flour
- 150g porridge oats
- 150g unsalted butter, at room temperature cut into small cubes
- 50g toasted whole hazelnuts

Method

1. Pre-heat the oven to 180°C. Place the sliced fruit in a large ovenproof dish, sprinkling each layer with some of the sugar and cinnamon.

2. In a large bowl mix together the flour, porridge oats and remaining sugar. Using your fingers rub in the butter until the mix appears like chunky breadcrumbs. You can also use a food processor to do this. Roughly mix the hazelnuts into the crumble.

3. Firmly press the crumble topping onto the fruit and sprinkle a little sugar on top.

4. Bake in the oven for 35 minutes or until golden brown and bubbling. Serve immediately with ice cream, yogurt or custard.

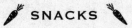

SNACKS

Rather than raiding the biscuit tin or tucking in a chocolate bar, try these easy and healthy snacks which also taste great.

HONEY FRUIT AND NUT FLAPJACKS

Makes 8/10 bars

Ingredients

- 8oz butter
- 3oz sugar
- 2tbsp runny honey
- 300g porridge oats
- 100g dried raisins, apricots, cranberries – chocolate chips can be added as an alternative
- 50g chopped mixed nuts

Method

1. Pre-heat the oven to 180°C and grease an 8-inch baking tin. In a pan melt the butter, sugar and runny honey.

2. Mix the oats, fruit and nuts into the mixture, ensuring an even coat. Press firmly into the tin and bake in the oven for 25 minutes or until golden brown. If you prefer softer flapjacks you can cook for less time or for crunchier flapjacks add 5 minutes to the cooking time.

3. Allow to cool in the tin and then cut into squares and set on a wire rack. The flapjacks can be stored for several days in an airtight container.

CHOC CHIP BANANA AND WALNUT BREAD

Ingredients

- 3 or 4 large ripe bananas – the more bananas you use the more moist and heavy the bread

- 200g wholemeal flour – you could use plain white flour but wholemeal is healthier and gives the bread a nice grainy texture

- 100g soft margarine or butter, also for greasing tin

- ½ tsp salt

- ½ tsp ground nutmeg

- 100g Demerara sugar

- 1 large egg beaten

- 1tbsp baking powder

- 75g chopped walnuts

- 50g raisins

- 50g dark chocolate chips – these can easily be left out if you don't want chocolate in the bread.

Method

1. Pre-heat the oven to 180°C and grease a loaf tin.

2. Mash the bananas until smooth – either by hand or using an electric hand whisk.

3. Cream together the margarine, sugar, banana, egg, baking powder and sieve the flour into the mixture. Stir rigorously and add the walnuts, raisins and choc chips. If the mixture seems too dry a drop of milk can be added at this stage.

4. Transfer to the loaf tin and bake for 45–60 minutes. The bread is cooked when the top feels springy and a skewer inserted in the middle of the bread comes away clean. Run a knife along the side of the bread and leave to cook on a wire rack.

🥕 COOKING FOR NON-VEGGIES 🥕

Most meat-eaters enjoy vegetarian food. From delicious pasta dishes to fragrant curries to spicy Asian noodles, cooking for non-veggies is easy.

Here are a few ideas of dishes to cook for a meat-eater who is a little unsure of vegetarian cooking:

- three bean chilli with rice and tacos
- roasted vegetable lasagne
- vegetable paella
- vegetable curry with rice and naan bread
- spinach and ricotta cannelloni.

TIPS ON ADAPTING NON-VEGETARIAN RECIPES

- If you had a tried and tested favourite meat dish that you enjoyed eating before you became a vegetarian or fancy adapting a traditional meat dish, rest assured it is easier to do than you may think.

- Don't be afraid to play around with the ingredients as there is no need to follow a recipe by the book, for example adding blended vegetables to a pasta sauce. Adding extra vegetables is a good way to bulk up a dish. You can also change the texture of the vegetable by slicing, dicing, peeling, grating or mashing.

- Another way to adapt meat dishes is to supplement the meat with vegetarian alternative products or add grains, pulses, nuts and seeds to the dish to create more interesting flavours and textures.

Some traditional dishes that can be adapted easily are listed below.

- **Cottage pie:** vegetarian mince or roasted vegetables can be used to replace the meat mince and the traditional recipe can be followed.

- **Chilli con carne:** either use mixed beans or vegetarian mince to create a vegetarian alternative.

- **Lasagne:** vegetarian mince can be used as can roasted vegetables.

- **Double cheese beef burgers:** try drizzling a large Portobello mushroom with olive oil and crumble a little blue cheese on top, season with pepper and grill or oven bake until cooked. Serve in a wholemeal bun with sliced tomatoes and crunchy lettuce.

- **Sausage and mash:** a pack of veggie sausages and hearty homemade onion gravy provides a good vegetarian alternative and is easy to adapt.

- **Toad in the hole:** veggie sausages can be used to replace the meat sausages.

- **Sunday roast:** a homemade or bought nut roast can be used to replace a roast chicken or beef. Alternatively, try slicing a large red pepper in half and stuffing with vegetarian stuffing mix and roasting in the oven for around 20 minutes.

RECIPES FOR SPECIAL OCCASIONS

Food plays an important role in special occasions such as Christmas, Easter and the simple family get together over a Sunday Roast. As a vegetarian there is no reason that celebratory meals shouldn't be that extra bit special. It is natural to have some nostalgia for traditional dishes such as turkey at Christmas or burgers and sausages on the BBQ, and you may have some apprehensions about how vegetarian alternatives will measure up. Here are a few ideas to show you how to celebrate special occasions with a vegetarian meal that won't leave you feeling like you've missed out.

VEGETARIAN CHRISTMAS

On Christmas Day why not opt for one of these tasty vegetarian alternatives that can be bought ready-made or made at home.

Turkey alternatives

- Vegetarian nut roast with cranberry and mulled wine sauce.

- Quorn turkey-style roast with stuffing.

- Roasted red peppers filled with a nut and sage stuffing.

Roast potatoes

To create the perfect vegetarian roast potato, first peel and quarter the potatoes. Next heat the oil in a baking tray – sunflower or vegetable oil is fine. As the oil is heating season and coat the potatoes with salt, pepper and sprinkle with a spoonful of white flour. Shake rigorously and carefully place in the tray. Top with fresh rosemary and cook until golden brown and crispy at 220°C.

Pocket tip ⚓

Many chefs roast potatoes in goose fat at Christmas to add flavour and make the potatoes extra crispy. Obviously, as a vegetarian you want to avoid this so if you are eating out it is best to check.

Roast vegetables

Vegetables should feature heavily in a Christmas dinner so there is no reason to prepare alternatives if you are a mixed group of vegetarians and non-vegetarians.

Pocket tip ❖

If you hate plain old boiled Brussels sprouts then try roasting in the oven with garlic, rosemary, salt, pepper, olive oil and a handful of toasted almonds for tasty sprouts with a bit more bite.

VEGETARIAN EASTER

Hot cross buns and Easter eggs aside, here are a couple of vegetarian meal ideas to help you celebrate Easter.

Lamb alternatives

- Roasted vegetable stacks with grilled halloumi cheese served with couscous and fresh bread.
- Vegetable stew.
- Vegetable pie with mash potatoes and peas and onion gravy.

SUNDAY ROAST

With our increasingly busy lives it is no wonder that the traditional Sunday Roast lunch is a meal most people enjoy. Vegetarians can still enjoy Sunday lunch with one of these tasty alternatives:

- nut roast with roast potatoes and vegetables
- vegetarian shepherd's pie
- vegetable rice gratin.

BBQS

As a vegetarian you can still enjoy the summer BBQ season. Veggie bean, nut and vegetable burgers, and vegetarian sausages barbeque well and are filling and satisfying. If you are going to a friend's house for a BBQ why not take along a selection of vegetarian burgers and salads to share?

THE VEGETARIAN WEDDING

For vegetarian couples planning on tying the knot it is unlikely that you will want to serve meat at your wedding.

With a little of creative thought a vegetarian wedding menu can be exciting and attractive to meat-eaters as well as vegetarians and there are catering companies springing up all over the place that offer vegetarian catering services. A good way to satisfy non-vegetarians is to offer a rice or pasta dish. Wines can also be carefully chosen to ensure they are vegetarian.

It is surprisingly easy to throw a vegetarian wedding breakfast. Here's a sample menu:

- starter: tomato and basil soup or carrot and coriander with a roll

- main: creamy spinach gnocchi or wild mushroom and truffle oil risotto

- sides: roasted vegetables or a rocket and tomato salad

- dessert: chocolate torte or blueberry and vanilla crème brûlée.

VEGGIE AND VEGAN COOKBOOKS

These are some of the best vegetarian and vegan cookbooks to get you inspired and cooking up a storm in the kitchen.

Plenty: Vibrant Recipes from London's Ottolenghi
Yotam Ottolenghi
Published by Chronicle Books

The popular London eatery has been wowing diners for some time now and its Head Chef has been helping vegetarians with his weekly column in the *Guardian*. This cookbook unites the two projects with simple, clean recipes from Ottolenghi's personal collection.

Appetite for Reduction: 125 Fast and Filling Low-Fat Vegan Recipes
Isa Chandra Moskowitz
Published by Da Capo Press

This book contains around 100 low-calorie yet delicious and generous recipes designed to help you lose weight.

Sarah Raven's Garden Cookbook
Sarah Raven
Published by Bloomsbury Publishing

This book isn't exclusively vegetarian but contains many vegetarian recipes which will be great when cooking for a mixed audience. This is a practical, wholesome volume which will appeal to fans of Hugh Fearnley-Whittingstall. Sarah Raven's experience at the River Cafe shines through in an excellent collection of comforting recipes.

Rose Eliot's New Complete Vegetarian
Rose Eliot
Published by Collins

Timeless classics and modern inventions from the most established British vegetarian chef. This is an essential book for the vegetarian kitchen which will provide a constant source of reference.

Step-by-Step Vegetarian Cookbook
Good Housekeeping
Published by Ebury

A beginner's book which nonetheless has an international inspiration and draws from a wide range of recipes. It is a great book to buy for those just starting out with a vegetarian lifestyle.

Eat Vegetarian
Sam Stern
Published by Walker

Fast, simple, delicious vegetarian food as can be expected from this young chef. If you're a fan of Jamie Oliver's style, then you'll appreciate this accessible and practical cookbook.

La Dolce Vegan! Vegan Livin' Made Easy
Sarah Kramer
Published by Arsenal Pulp Press

This is a bubbly and inventive book which offers sage advice on all aspects of vegan living, not only recipes. The recipes it does provide, however, are delicious and inspiring with a real DIY ethic.

The New Moosewood Cookbook
Mollie Katzen
Published by Ten Speed Press

One of America's best-loved chefs who has consistently set the standard in accessible cookery books. These natural, healthy recipes are charmingly illustrated and will provide great inspiration for beginners and long-time vegetarians alike.

The Asian Vegan Kitchen: Authentic and Appetizing Dishes from the Continent of Rich Flavors
Hema Parekh
Published by Kodansha International

The author was born in India before moving to Japan and this Pan-Asian character is reflected in this eclectic and interesting vegetarian recipe book. Soups, noodles, curries and all manner of Asian dishes will delight the more adventurous vegetarian chef.

Veganomicon: The Ultimate Vegan Cookbook
Isa Chandra Moskowitz
Published by Da Capo Press

A passionate and inventive book which is a gem for beginners and experienced chefs alike. Moskowitz is a committed vegan and really outlines the basics of vegan cooking in this essential reference work.

6

EATING OUT

The number of vegetarian restaurants, cafes and menu options has grown considerably during the past 10–15 years, as more people choose to adopt a healthy vegetarian lifestyle. While some countries are more challenging than others in terms of finding many, if any, vegetarian options in restaurants, even the most meat heavy countries are now realising that it is always worth having at least one vegetarian option on the menu. See p.126 for more on vegetarian cuisine while travelling.

Pocket fact 🌶

The UK has seen a 50% increase in gourmet vegetarian restaurants since 2007, bringing the number of high-end vegetarian restaurants in Britain to 30.

🥕 HOW TO DECIPHER THE MENU 🥕

Many menus today come with a vegetarian or vegan symbol, generally 'V' for vegetarian and 'VG' for vegan. Most chain restaurants in Western countries also include information on whether the dish contains nuts or is suitable for people with certain allergies. Menus today do make picking a vegetarian option easier, but remember, if in doubt, you can always ask your waiter or waitress to double-check.

HOW TO ASK ABOUT INGREDIENTS

Don't be afraid to ask exactly what ingredients a dish contains. Many recipes will contain 'hidden' products that are animal derived and you may not be able to taste them in the dish itself. Most chefs won't mind being asked and it may be possible to make the same dish without the animal product being used.

Commonly used in some dishes are animal-derived ingredients such as fish oil, meat stock, gelatine and anchovies, parmesan cheese and some wines, which you may not easily be able to detect, but would probably rather not eat as a vegetarian! If you're ever in doubt just ask.

WHAT TO ORDER IN RESTAURANTS

Vegetarian restaurants

If you are lucky enough to be eating at a vegetarian or vegan restaurant then the menu is your oyster; vegetarian oyster of course! Going to a vegetarian restaurant is a great way to discover new dishes and seek inspiration for your own cooking and meal planning. Vegetarian chefs are increasingly pushing the boundaries of vegetarian cuisine further as they explore new ways of cooking to create a delectable vegetarian feast.

Non-vegetarian restaurants

While some non-vegetarian restaurants don't always offer much of a choice for vegetarians, or are unimaginative about their offerings it is becoming less acceptable for vegetarians not to be catered for properly. An unadventurous macaroni cheese or baked potato just doesn't cut it as the vegetarian option nowadays, particularly as many meat-eaters also enjoy vegetarian food. This hasn't gone unnoticed by top chefs, who are adding a greater number of vegetarian dishes to their menus.

Italian restaurants

A lot of Italian dishes are suitable for vegetarians, provided you eat dairy and/or eggs. Good options to choose include the following.

- Basil and tomato penne: made from fresh or tinned tomatoes, onion and garlic to create a rich tomato sauce and seasoned with salt, pepper and fresh basil.

- Classic margherita pizza: a classic pizza dough base made of flour, egg and milk, with a tomato and basil sauce and mozzarella cheese topping.

- Fungi pizza: pizza topped with mushrooms and cheese.

Pocket fact 🖋

The first Vegetarian Britain guide published in 1998 featured 270 vegetarian establishments. The fourth edition features around 450 establishments, plus many more wholefood shops, and spans 800 pages. For more information and where to buy, visit www. vegetarianguides.co.uk.

French restaurants

The choice in French restaurants is a bit limited for vegetarians as the French diet contains a lot of meat and fish. For vegetarians who eat dairy and/or eggs there is some choice, but for those on more restrictive diets French restaurants are probably best avoided where possible.

You could try the following classic options.

- Goat's cheese salad: toasted French bread topped with grilled goat's cheese, placed on a bed of salad and drizzled with French dressing.

- Classic French crêpe: a savoury pancake filled with grated cheese and often served with green salad and French bread.

- French omelette: made simply with eggs, a little butter and fresh herbs such as parsley or chives.

Japanese restaurants

The Japanese diet may be rich in fish served either raw as sashimi or wrapped in rice as sushi but also includes a good range of vegetarian and vegan dishes containing tofu and vegetables. If you fancy trying Japanese cuisine, here are some suggestions.

- Soba noodles with vegetable tempura: buckwheat noodles served hot or cold with a plate of piping hot vegetable tempura.

- Udon: white noodles served in a broth – you may need to request that no shrimp is added.

- Sushi: cucumber and egg sushi dishes are commonly found.

Pocket fact 🌶

The island of Okinawa off the coast of Japan is said to have one of the longest life expectancies in the world, accredited to the traditional diet high in soya, legumes and vegetables, and low in fat. Very little meat, except small amounts of pork, and occasionally fish, dairy, and eggs are eaten.

Thai restaurants

Thai cuisine is a complex blend of spicy, sour, salty and sweet flavours. Commonly used ingredients include lemongrass, chilli (be warned some Thai dishes are extremely hot!), coriander, mint and garlic. For vegetarians, egg and several types of tofu are used in noodle, rice and curry dishes.

You might find the following dishes are a good option.

- Vegetable phat Thai: fried noodles, bean sprouts, chillies, peanuts, sliced carrot, pepper, eggs and tofu. If you don't eat eggs just ask for it without.

- Phat phak khanaa: stir-fried Chinese green vegetables with garlic and soy sauce.

- Vegetable Thai green or red curry: a fragrant curry dish made with coconut milk, lemongrass, chilli and vegetables such as aubergine, peppers and tofu. It can have quite a kick so ask for a milder curry if you don't want it super hot.

- Vegetable spring rolls: bean sprouts, shredded carrot and glass noodles in a crisp spring roll, served with a chilli dipping sauce.

Pocket tip ⚜

A pungent fish sauce is often used in Thai cooking, so you'll need to clearly request that it is left out when ordering food.

Indian restaurants

Authentic southern Indian cuisine is predominantly vegetarian as vegetables, lentils and pulses play an integral part in Indian cooking. Most vegetarians find Indian food a unique culinary experience in that there is so much vegetarian food on offer. Indian restaurants offer an excellent range of options for vegetarians and if you're not keen on spicy curries milder options are available.

- Palak paneer: a mild and healthy curry made with spinach and baked cottage cheese, which provides an excellent source of protein.

- Dhal: a lentil-based curry with chillies and spices.

- Vegetable korma: this is a mild dish with vegetables and cream.

- Samosa: potato and vegetable-filled deep fried pastry.

- Onion bhaji: onions mixed with flour and spices and deep fried.

Greek restaurants

Traditional Greek cooking uses fresh seasonal vegetables, fruits, grains, olives, pulses, herbs, spices, and olive oil, all of which are perfect for vegetarians. Feta cheese and eggs also feature quite heavily, so for vegetarians who eat dairy and eggs there is a slightly wider choice.

The following are popular vegetarian choices.

- Greek salad: feta cheese, lettuce, fresh tomatoes, cucumber, red onion and basil with an olive oil and balsamic vinegar dressing.

- Moussaka: a traditional Greek dish made with sliced potatoes, aubergines and either lamb or beef in a rich tomato sauce. However, vegetarian alternatives are often available using mushrooms instead. The dish is topped with a creamy white sauce.

- Spanakopita: a spinach, onion and feta pie in filo pastry.

- Hummus: a traditional Greek dip made with blended chick-peas, tahini (sesame paste), garlic, olive oil, salt and pepper.

- Tzatziki: a yogurt, cucumber and mint dip.

- Stuffed vine leaves: rice with herbs, spices and olive oil wrapped in a vine leaf.

- Pitta bread: traditional Greek flat bread commonly eaten with dips.

Pocket fact

Greek 'meze' — a variety of small dishes to share — offers a good selection for vegetarians, such as Greek bruschetta, hummus, feta and spinach filo pastries, olives, cold marinated aubergine salad and tabbouleh.

BRITAIN'S BEST VEGETARIAN RESTAURANTS

From the humble veggie cafe to the gourmet London dining establishment, here are some of Britain's finest vegetarian places to eat.

MILDRED'S

Mildred's serves an internationally inspired range of vegetarian and vegan food. Established in 1988 Mildred's offers friendly service in a lively atmosphere and is excellent value for money for a central London location.

- **Menu description:** An eclectic mix of dishes, many of which are gluten- and wheat-free. From stews to curries to Asian cuisine and salads the menu offers a range of dishes from across the globe. The pudding list is also divine and most of the desserts are suitable for vegans.

- **Location:** Soho, London.

- **Website:** www.mildreds.co.uk.

- **Price range:** Expect to pay around £10 for a main meal. Organic and non-organic wines start at £15.90 a bottle.

TERRE À TERRE

Award-winning vegetarian restaurant Terre à Terre was founded in 1993, by Amanda Powley and Philip Taylor who work hard to push the boundaries of vegetarian food and create innovate, delicious recipes.

- **Menu description:** With dishes such as Terre à tiffin thali, it's hard to find a more exotic vegetarian menu.

- **Location:** Brighton.

- **Website:** www.terreaterre.co.uk.

- **Price range:** Expect to pay around £14.95 for a main meal on the à la carte menu, or £30 for a three-course party menu. Wine starts at £17.20 a bottle.

VANILLA BLACK

Originally established in York in 2004, Vanilla Black relocated to London in 2008 where it quickly gained a reputation as one of London's top vegetarian gourmet restaurants, even achieving a Michelin recommendation.

- **Menu description:** Vanilla Black's cuisine is as far from a humble veggie cafe offering as vegetarian food can be, with dishes such as fried mushroom mousse and tarragon waffles or warm blue cheese pannacotta and charred celery.

- **Location:** London, nearest tube Chancery Lane.
- **Website:** www.vanillablack.co.uk.
- **Price range:** The two- and three-course menus offer outstanding value for money, considering the high standard of the food and service. A two- course lunch and dinner meal costs £24.50 and the three course £32.50 a person.

TIBITS

Serving healthy fast-food vegetarian food in buffet style, Tibits is one of the best places to grab a vegetarian meal on the go. This is part of an international chain of restaurants linked to the Hiltl restaurant in Zurich. The first Tibits restaurant opened in Switzerland in 2000 and in London a couple of years later.

- **Menu description:** A hearty mix of homemade sandwiches, soups and stews, or build your own meal by picking from over 40 dishes in the buffet, inspired by Indian, Asian and Mediterranean cooking.
- **Location:** London, near Regent's Street.
- **Website:** www.tibits.co.uk.
- **Price range:** You can choose from the eat in or take out option. Meals are buffet style and priced according to weight. On average plates cost around £7.50 for lunch.

HERBIES

One of the veggie gems of the South West, Herbies has been feeding the West Country's vegetarians and vegans for more than 20 years.

- **Menu description:** Rustic vegetarian food at its best. From hearty homemade nut and bean burgers and falafels that are so filling they will keep you going for hours, to vegetable bakes, pastas and curries, this is a good place to come to get inspired by vegetarian food that you could recreate at home. A good selection of vegetarian and vegan cakes, puddings and ice creams are also sold, alongside organic beers, wines, teas and coffees.

- **Location:** Exeter, Devon.
- **Website:** None.
- **Price range**: Herbies is excellent value for money. Burgers and light bites come in at less than a fiver and main courses cost around £7.

THE 78

Scottish pubs are not traditionally associated with vegetarian food, however Glasgow's The 78 is a homely and cosy pub that serves a 100% vegetarian menu.

- **Menu description:** While The 78 does serve hearty vegetarian pub grub such as veggie burger and a pint it also has some more inspired choices such as pan-fried Asian noodles, homemade curry, and a coconut and bean chilli wrap.
- **Location:** Glasgow, Scotland.
- **Website:** www.the78cafebar.com.
- **Price range:** The 78 is serious value for money, mains cost around £7.95, with lighter bites at around £5.

THE VEGETARIAN FOOD STUDIO

For vegetarian curry enthusiasts the award-winning Vegetarian Food Studio in Cardiff is the place to go as the entire menu consists of delicious vegetarian curries and side dishes.

- **Menu description:** An enormous menu consisting of traditional dishes from all over India. The menu includes tasty curry dishes made using vegetables, tofu, lentils and pulses.
- **Location:** Cardiff, Wales.
- **Website:** www.vegetarianfoodstudio.co.uk.
- **Price range:** Amazing value for money, expect to pay £4.95 for a main course and £2.95 for a side dish.

VEGGIE WORLD

This Milton Keynes-based company produces a range of take-home food as well as running a restaurant on-site. They pride themselves on welcoming meat-eaters who want to experiment with a vegan lifestyle and have a wide range of 'veggie burgers' and the like to help make the jump!

- **Menu description:** A copious menu of vegan Chinese dishes with a few vegetarian options to boot.

- **Location:** Milton Keynes, Buckinghamshire.

- **Website:** www.veggie-world.com/Restaurant.

- **Price range:** Extremely good value, with some of their take-away main dishes staring at £2.50.

THE RIVERSIDE VEGETARIA

The Riverside is a cosmopolitan restaurant on the banks of the Thames which is housed in a quirky green building on Kingston High Street. They have outside space and the ability to accommodate groups, so it's a perfect place to take friends for a meal.

- **Menu description:** Eclectic menu ranging from Caribbean casseroles to curries via nut roasts.

- **Location:** Kingston-upon-Thames, Surrey.

- **Website:** www.rsveg.plus.com.

- **Price range:** Mains cost around £8–£9.

EARTH CAFÉ

This bijou vegetarian cafe below the Buddhist Centre in Manchester is run along Buddhist principles.

- **Menu description:** They use organic and fair-trade food where possible and encourage the use of local products.

- **Location:** Manchester.

- **Website:** www.earthcafe.co.
- **Price range:** Very reasonably priced.

YUMMYV

Delightful fusion of Thai and Chinese foods with all the familiar sauces (like kung po, satay, etc) and some new dishes to try.

- **Menu description:** Extensive selection of Chinese dishes with an attractive Dim Sum menu.
- **Location:** Harrow.
- **Website:** www.yummyv.co.uk.
- **Price range:** Mains cost between £5–£6.

LAKELAND PEDLAR

This cafe and deli is situated at the gateway to the Lake District. Combining an international whole foods restaurant and a bike shop it embodies the quirky yet welcoming atmosphere of the Lake District.

- **Menu description:** Check out the website for some gorgeous photos of their whole food menu.
- **Location:** Keswick, Cumbria.
- **Website:** www.lakelandpedlar.co.uk.
- **Price range:** Well priced with a full meal for two coming in at under £25.

THE BLAKE HEAD VEGETARIAN CAFE

The Blake Head is a well-stocked and interesting book shop with everything from coffee-table books to children's classics. Their Vegetarian Cafe is open for breakfast and lunch, serving a variety of classic dishes alongside gourmet creations.

- **Menu description:** Classic breakfasts and daily lunchtime specials.

- **Location:** York.
- **Website:** www.theblakehead.co.uk.
- **Price range:** Breakfasts come in around £5 and lunch dishes are around £6.50.

THE LOVING HUT

This small chain of veggie restaurants across the South East is well worth a visit. Their 'eat what you like, pay what you like' buffet is great value and a great concept. Check out their website for some great food photography.

- **Menu description:** Delicious veggie comfort food like burgers and nuggets alongside well-made curries and soups.
- **Location:** Camden, Edgware, Archway, Brighton and Norwich.
- **Website:** www.risc.org.uk/globalcafe.
- **Price range:** Main meals around £5 or try the 'pay-what-you-feel' buffet.

MANNA VEGETARIAN RESTAURANT

High class cuisine which is prepared meticulously and served beautifully. A real taste-sensation which breaks the mould of 'veggie cafe' and presents a really tempting, top-notch vegetarian restaurant you'd be proud to take a critic to.

- **Menu description:** Up-market, creative veggie dishes.
- **Location:** Primrose Hill, London.
- **Website:** www.mannav.com.
- **Price range:** Starters are around £8 and mains £14.

INTERNATIONAL VEGETARIAN RESTAURANTS

Here's a selection of vegetarian and vegan restaurants around the world which you may come across on your travels. Some are well known and some less so, though they all come highly recommended.

HAUS HILTL

This central guest house and kitchen employs a large number of chefs to prepare high quality food from scratch. Their fresh daily menu offers great variety and great innovation.

- **Location:** Zurich, Switzerland.
- **Website:** www.hiltl.ch.

LA BÁSCULA

A co-operative cafe which has a large dining room built in a former chocolate factory. Its laid-back atmosphere offers the perfect setting for their selection of healthy vegetarian dishes and shakes.

- **Location:** Barcelona, Spain.
- **Website:** www.sincarne.net/barcelona-vegetarian-restaurants/la-bascula.htm.

COOKIES CREAM

A romantic and unique restaurant in Berlin hidden behind the Westin hotel with creative and interesting food with a different menu every weak. It can be expensive and isn't perfect for everyone, but offers something different and an exciting experience. Their website is pretty illuminating as to whether you'll love or hate this restaurant, stick with it and you'll eventually find the menu!

- **Location:** Berlin, Germany.
- **Website:** www.cookiescream.com.

PEACE 'N LOVE

A delightful cafe with a good range of vegan dishes and a welcoming ambience, although the opening hours are limited to lunch time.

- **Location:** Perpignan, France.
- **Website:** www.veggieheaven.com/europe/france/Peacen_love_6471.

CORNUCOPIA

This is Dublin's most established vegetarian cafe and it serves a great selection of veggie classics. It's very popular with locals and always dependable for a friendly atmosphere.

- **Location:** Dublin, Ireland.
- **Website:** www.cornucopia.ie.

DOLCE VEGAN

This is an organic bakery with a small restaurant attached which offers simple, yet delicious Italian food. Excellent value with good range of pastas, salads and mains.

- **Location:** Florence, Italy.
- **Website:** www.dolcevegan.it.

LE GRENIER DE NOTRE-DAME

A quaint left-bank restaurant which offers a variety of vegetarian and vegan options. Beautifully presented food and highly recommended juices.

- **Location:** Paris, France.
- **Website:** www.vegguide.org/entry/3497.

IL MARGUTTA VEGETARIANO

Rome's most famous vegetarian restaurant in a country in which it is often difficult to find specifically veggie food. It has a large vegan menu with many new and interesting dishes which you may not have come across.

- **Location:** Rome, Italy.
- **Website:** www.ilmarguttavegetariano.it.

ISLA DEL TESORO

This is a very popular, up-scale restaurant in the Spanish capital which has a varied and exciting menu. It is a favourite with tourists and locals alike.

- **Location:** Madrid, Spain.
- **Website:** www.isladeltesoro.net.

CLOSER

There's a friendly atmosphere in this restaurant by the beach, with recommended shakes and a great selection of coffees. They serve burgers, bagels and other vegetarian treats.

- **Location:** Cape Town, South Africa.
- **Website:** www.vegguide.org/entry/13722.

LAS VEGAN NIRVANA

Despite the Vegas word play, there's no gambling when it comes to this popular and friendly cafe. They were originally a bakery although began opening for lunch and now serve dinner on Thursdays and Fridays. Their Indonesian rice balls come highly recommended.

- **Location:** Melbourne, Australia.
- **Website:** www.myspace.com/lasveganbakery.

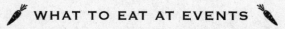

WHAT TO EAT AT EVENTS

Eating as a vegetarian at events can be challenging; however, it is possible to manage perfectly well provided you know what to look for and avoid.

BUFFETS

Buffets can be a minefield – you take a bite of the innocent-looking triangle of sandwich to find it contains hidden meat, or the quiche has strips of bacon. One way to avoid this is to ask a meat-eater to act as your official 'taster' and check whether dishes contain meat or not. Most people won't mind being asked and this can save you the unpleasant experience of getting an unwanted mouthful of meat! Make sure the taster knows if you don't eat fish as they may assume you do. Alternatively, just ask your host or waiter.

Pocket tip ❦

Carry a pack of dried fruit or nuts in your bag to help keep you going in case the vegetarian option is really limited.

Top five vegetarian buffet dishes

1. *Potato salad.*
2. *Rice or couscous salad.*
3. *Vegetable quiche.*
4. *Olive and tomato pasta salad.*
5. *Vegetable wraps or sandwiches.*

PRE-ORDERED MENUS

Pre-ordered menus at weddings, work functions or celebrations generally offer just one or two vegetarian options. While this can go in your favour if it is a dish you like, if it is something you can't eat then it is advisable to phone ahead in plenty of time to ask whether another option can be provided. Most establishments should be prepared and able to do this not just for vegetarians, but also for people with food allergies, intolerances and medical conditions. Remember you do need to let people know in advance of your diet.

If the vegetarian option is terrible

Soggy or overcooked vegetables, rubbery cheese or a bland uninspiring dish: yes, at some time or another as a vegetarian – or indeed as a meat-eater – we are all faced with a truly terrible meal.

If you find a vegetarian option is something you just can't eat, don't be afraid to ask if an alternative option can be provided – most chefs can easily whip up a simple vegetarian dish that will consist of ingredients you are happy eating and, most importantly, enjoy.

Unfortunately, there may be times when you may have to eat the vegetarian option, even if it's terrible. However, it's important to put this into perspective and remember it's just one meal and that the next one could be far better.

To ensure that you arrive to find a dish you enjoy eating ring ahead to order something specific. This way the chef can be prepared and you can avoid embarrassment or an awkward situation in front of friends, family or colleagues.

VEGETARIAN FOOD ON THE GO

Travelling as a vegetarian can open your eyes, mind and stomach to new and exciting foods and help broaden your palate. Unfortunately, at times, eating out while on holiday, commuting or on business trips can be a little trickier for vegetarians. The good news is that finding interesting places to eat out as a vegetarian is becoming increasingly diverse and the vast majority of the time a vegetarian and possibly a vegan option will be offered. This section provides some advice on dealing with these more challenging situations so that you can still enjoy your trip and the local culture and cuisine. With a little research and forward planning it is possible to travel the world as a vegetarian and find great places to eat to suit a variety of budgets and tastes. You just need to have a sense of adventure, a little patience and a bit of good humour!

COMMUTER FOOD

Pre-packaged airline food is never great whether you're a vegetarian or meat-eater, although many airlines are waking up to the fact that people expect more when travelling, and are continually looking to improve their food by enlisting the help of top chefs from around the world.

Pocket tip 🌱

Pack some vegetarian snacks: this could simply be a bag of dried fruit and nuts, fruit, vegetable sticks and dip, pitta breads or oat cakes and peanut butter.

When travelling by plane, it is important that you request your vegetarian meal well in advance, preferably when you book your ticket. This way you will avoid going hungry or having to make do with a meat dish if the crew run out of the vegetarian option before they reach you. Another advantage of being a vegetarian is that generally the vegetarian or special diet meals on a plane are served first, so you may find you are the envy of other passengers as they wait to be served!

Pocket tip 🌱

Take dried vegetarian foods with you: this way you can at least eat something to keep you going if the vegetarian option is poor. Dried instant soup, pasta, rice, noodle and soya products are light to carry and only take a minute or two to rehydrate with boiling water.

RESEARCHING VEGETARIAN OPTIONS ABROAD

As with any trip abroad it is worth doing your research. Buy local guides, surf the net and follow word of mouth advice and recommendations for the best places to stay, see and eat. If you think that you may have trouble finding vegetarian options or have a slightly pickier vegetarian in your party, it may be worth staying in self-catering accommodation as opposed to fully catered as this way you have more control over your meals. This is also a great way to cut costs and a chance to explore the local supermarket or market.

VEGETARIAN TERMS AND PHRASES TO USE ABROAD

While abroad it can help to be aware of the key terms and phrases used to describe both vegetarian and meat dishes.

French phrases

As France is rather a meat heavy country it is very useful for vegetarians to learn how to explain they are a vegetarian and some common words of animal products that you want to avoid. This is because some French restaurants have less strict interpretations of vegetarianism and may think it's acceptable to offer a vegetarian a dish that contains animal by-products such as rennet, gelatine or lard, provided it has no visible meat.

In French, vegetarian is *végétarien* and vegan is *végétalien*. Some useful phrases are listed below.

- I am a vegetarian = *Je suis végétarien/végétarienne.*

- I am a vegan = *Je suis végétalien/végétalienne.*

- Do you have a vegetarian option? = *Servez-vous des plats végétariens?*

- Does that have meat or fish in it? = *Est-ce que cela contient . . . de la viande?/du poisson?/des graisses animales? (animal fats).*

- I can't eat meat or fish = *Je ne peux pas manger de viande/de poisson.*

- I never eat meat or fish = *Je ne prends jamais de viande/de poisson.*

- I don't eat dairy or eggs = *Je ne mange pas de produits laitiers/Je ne mange pas d'oeufs.*

Words for animal products you want to avoid.

- *La présure* = rennet.
- *La gelatine* = gelatine.
- *Le saindoux* = lard.
- *Le cartilage* = gristle.
- *Le poil* = bristle.

Pocket fact 🌶

Rennet is sourced from an animal's (commonly cows, sheep and goats) stomach and is commonly used in the manufacturing process of some cheese making as it helps the milk to curdle. There are non-rennet cheeses readily available for vegetarians and vegans, but it is always worth checking the label of cheeses to see whether rennet is used.

Spanish phrases
Here are some useful phrases to have to hand while travelling in Spanish-speaking countries.

- I'm a vegetarian/vegan = *Soy vegetariano/soy un vegetariano estricto.*
- Do you have a vegetarian option? = *Tiene la optión para vegetarianos?*
- Does that have meat or fish in it? = *Contiene/tiene carne o pescado?*
- I can't eat meat/fish = *No puedo comer carne/pescado.*
- I don't eat dairy or eggs = *No como productos lacteos o huevas.*

- Animal fat = *grasa animal.*

- Gravy = *salsa.*

- Stock = *caldo.*

- Veggie burger = *hamburgesa vegetal.*

Japanese phrases

With a little explanation most restaurants in Japan can easily make a vegetarian option and are happy to do so. Vegetarians and vegans who don't eat meat or fish can easily get protein from tofu and other bean products. Soya is also commonly used.

Here are a few useful phrases.

- I'm a vegetarian = *Watashi wa bejitarian desu.*

- I'm a vegan (there is no Japanese word for vegan, so it is better so say you don't eat meat and dairy products) and don't eat meat or dairy = *Watashi wa saishoku shugisha desu kara niku ya nyuseihin wa tabenmasen.*

- I don't eat fish = *Shiifudo wa tabenmasen.*

- Do you have any vegetarian options? = *Bejitarian ryori ga arimasu ka?*

Chinese (Mandarin) phrases

In China, vegetarianism has been at the heart of its history and although most Chinese people eat a diet rich in meat, in the poorer rural parts of China a vegetarian diet or one with very small quantities of meat is still followed.

The only way to say you are a vegetarian has quite strong religious connotations, so it is better to say you don't eat meat.

Here are some handy phrases.

- I'm a vegetarian = *Wo ci zhai.*

- I don't eat meat = *Wo bu chi rou.*

- I don't eat . . . = *Wo bu chi . . .*
- I don't eat eggs = *Wo bu chi ji dan.*
- I don't eat fish = *Wo bu chi yu.*

Thai phrases

Thai food can be great for vegetarians and vegans as it is easily adaptable, so the meat can be left out. However, it is useful to make sure you are clearly understood when you order a meal so these simple phrases should help.

- I'm a vegetarian = *Chan/pom* [female/male] *gin mang-sa-wi-rat.*
- I don't want meat = *Mai sai neua-sa.*
- I don't want fish = *Mai sai plah.*
- Does this dish have meat in it? = *Aa-haan jaan nee mee neua sat mai?*
- Do you have any vegetarian food? = *Tee nee mee aa-haan mang-sa-wi-rat mai?*

Major vegetarian and vegan festivals and events

There are a number of excellent vegetarian and vegan festivals throughout the year and across the globe. Here is a small selection of some of the best.

- **London Vegan Festival** *takes place in Kensington Town Hall with hundreds of stalls promoting veganism, animal welfare, live music and crafts. The festival provides a lot of information on things taking place in the capital as well as activities for children and informative talks on different aspects of vegan living.*
- **The Phuket Vegetarian Festival** *is an annual event held in Phuket, Thailand during the ninth lunar month of the*

Chinese calendar. The festival is thought to be a good luck omen for religious observers with a whole host of accompanying sacred rituals. Locals ensure they stick to a strict 10 day vegan or vegetarian diet before performing amazing rituals like walking over hot coals or even climbing bladed ladders!

- **The West Midlands Vegan Festival** is held in Wolverhampton civic hall every year and welcomes all visitors (including non-vegans). Vegan producers and organisations set up stall alongside ethical companies to help promote healthy, cruelty-free, eco-friendly living.

- **VeggieFest** takes place just outside Chicago, USA. It combines international food stalls with live music and children's activities. This annual event is free to attend and well worth a visit.

- **VegfestUK, Bristol, UK** is a free, annual vegetarian food event boasting up to 100 stalls celebrating the vegan lifestyle including food, body care, fashion, campaigners, charities, cookery demonstrations, live music and films. For more information, visit www.bristol.vegfest.co.uk.

- **LA Vegan Beer Fest** is a unique event which showcases the impressive and delicious products of California's Vegan breweries, with beers from Sierra Nevada, Hangar 24 and many, many more.

- **Veggie Pride Paris, France** is, for a country that has a vegetarian population of just 2%, a surprisingly lively event. Vegetarians and vegans march first through the city of Paris to raise awareness. There are also food stands, talks and live music and entertainment.

- **The Boston Vegetarian Food Festival** runs annually in Massachusetts in the United States and brings together vegetarians from all over the East Coast to meet producers, try new products and listen to speakers from all over the world.

- **Vegan Festival Adelaide** takes place every year in beautiful South Australia. There are stalls from animal welfare organisations, environmentalists, organic producers and tastings of vegan food.
- **IVU World Vegetarian Congress, San Francisco, USA**, hosted by the San Francisco Vegetarian Society for a number of years, is a meeting where vegetarians discusses a number of issues related to vegetarianism.

7

CHILDREN AND VEGETARIANISM

Vegetarian diets are gaining popularity in families with children, as parents strive to ensure their children receive the best possible diet and nutrition, particularly in light of the five a day fruit and vegetable guidance. Children are often brought up vegetarian if one, or both, parents are already vegetarian, as it is easier for the whole family to eat the same diet. But for parents who are not vegetarian it may come as a surprise to discover just how strongly children can form views about vegetarianism and a child's wish to be vegetarian can raise worries. If your family isn't vegetarian, you might find it helpful to discover why your child wants to become a vegetarian and how to handle this change.

This chapter will provide comprehensive advice on bringing children up as vegetarians and help alleviate any concerns you may have about doing so. Rest assured, fed correctly, vegetarian children will be as full of beans – possibly quite literally – and as healthy, if not more so, than children eating meat.

VEGETARIAN CHILDREN'S NUTRITIONAL NEEDS

As any parent understands, it is crucial that a growing child's nutritional needs are met to ensure healthy physical development and growth. Choosing a vegetarian diet for yourself as a grown adult is one thing, but deciding to bring up your children as vegetarian is quite another.

While plenty of nutritional evidence and trained nutritionists agree that a wholesome and varied vegetarian diet does fulfil the nutritional needs of a child it is important to consider a vegetarian diet for children very carefully, as while an adult's diet only needs to maintain bodily functions, children's diets must fulfil two important processes: the maintenance of bodily functions and the support of healthy growth. Bringing children up as vegetarians is perfectly healthy and safe, but parents of vegetarian children need to ensure that their nutritional needs are met.

Pocket tip ✠
You should always consult a doctor before deciding to radically alter your child's diet.

Vegetarian children who eat and drink dairy products and eggs should have no problem getting the bulk of the protein and omega nutrients that they need. When coupled with a vegetarian diet rich in fruit and vegetables, lentils and pulses, and wholegrains they are unlikely to lack anything.

However, if vegetarian children don't eat dairy or eggs, they need to eat larger amounts of vegetarian foods to ensure they get the nutrients and calories they need. Encourage vegetarian children to eat as wide a variety of vegetarian food as possible, rather than just junk food – this will ensure they are not lacking in any nutrients or minerals.

A poorly planned vegetarian diet commonly lacks protein, calcium, iron, zinc and the vitamin B12, which can seriously affect a child's health. A good way to boost your child's intake of these nutrients is to feed them healthy breakfast cereals or soya milks, as these are usually fortified with vitamins and minerals. It's a good idea to avoid sugary or chocolaty cereals and only offer these as a treat.

Pocket tip 🏵

To get the benefit from fortified breakfast cereals, encourage your child to drink the milk they have poured over their cereal as it will contain the bulk of the vitamins. This is because, in order to coat them thoroughly, the cereal is sprayed with fortified vitamins and minerals which wash off when milk is added.

The following sections will provide advice on how to ensure that growing vegetarian children receive all of the essential nutrients they need. (For more information on adult and older vegetarian children's nutritional needs, see Chapter 2).

AMINO ACIDS

While our bodies can produce some types of amino acids on its own, there are 10 'essential' amino acids that we can only get from the food we eat:

- phenylalanine

- valine

- tryptophan

- threonine

- isoleucine

- methionine

- lysine

- leucine

- histidine

- arginine.

Histidine and arginine are the two amino acids that are essential for children to ensure their bodies absorb the necessary nutrients they need to grow. Histidine is an essential part of haemoglobin (a protein responsible for carrying oxygen in the blood) and arginine (an amino acid which is a basic component of protein) is vital for muscle growth and tissue repair. Try to give your children a variety of plant foods, grains, soya products, nuts and seeds, nut butters, meat alternatives, and beans each day. This way you can be sure that they will get all of the essential protein and amino acids that they need.

CALCIUM

Most of us know that dairy milk contains calcium which is important for growing and maintaining healthy bones and teeth, particularly important in children. However, there are alternative sources which ovo-vegetarians or vegan children need to consume to avoid any deficiency, including:

- calcium-fortified soya or rice milk
- tofu
- baked beans
- chickpeas and hummus
- kidney beans
- dark green leafy vegetables such as spinach, curly kale, broccoli
- almonds
- tahini (sesame seed paste)
- sesame seeds
- malt extract such as Marmite or equivalent.

IRON

It is vital that children get enough iron in their diets. A lack of iron is known as anaemia and can be a common problem in young girls going through puberty or those who have started menstruation and eating a restricted diet. While iron is plentiful in red meat, a whole host of vegetables and vegetarian foods also provide a good source, including:

- dark green leafy vegetables, such as broccoli and spinach
- dried apricots and raisins
- dried beans such as chickpeas, lentils, kidney beans, etc.
- iron-fortified breakfast cereals and breads.

Pocket fact

Foods high in vitamin C, eg citrus fruits such as oranges, lemons and kiwis, help enhance the body's absorption of iron. So try to combine foods rich in vitamin C with iron-dense foods in a meal to maximise its nutritional value.

VITAMIN B12

If you are concerned that your child may be lacking in this essential vitamin, fortified foods are a good way to boost their levels. Breakfast cereals, soya milk and some fruit juices are all a good source. Vitamin B12 tablets can also be taken and are available from all health food stores.

Pocket fact

Studies have shown children who eat a healthy breakfast perform better in school as they are more alert and can concentrate better than a child who has skipped breakfast.

IF YOUR CHILD IS A FUSSY EATER

It is important that all children eat fruit and vegetables; however, if your child is a vegetarian then it is even more important that they eat a wide range of fruit and vegetables. If your child is a fussy eater and won't eat their greens, there is still a whole host of ways you can 'trick' them into eating fruit and vegetables, eggs, lentils, tofu and so on.

A few tried and tested ways you can disguise foods they claim to 'hate' are listed below.

- **Mashing or blending to disguise the appearance of the food.** For example, if a child claims to dislike a certain type of fruit or vegetable then blending it into a drink, sauce, smoothie or soup is an excellent way to get the nutrients into their diet without a mealtime showdown and tears.

- **Adding to a food they love.** For example, if your child enjoys eating pizza or veggie burgers then adding a few cleverly chopped vegetables on top or to a salad means they may eat them without noticing. Using fresh tomatoes to make a pasta sauce or sneaking a few peas or sweetcorn into a dish like macaroni cheese is a good way to hide extra vegetables.

- **Packing or presenting the food in a way they will find exciting or entertaining.** Packaging food in a fun lunch box or fast-food type container can often encourage a child to eat. Chopping fruit or vegetables into child bite-sized pieces or arranging them in a fun way on the plate, such as faces or stars, can help distract from the fact you are feeding them fruit or vegetables.

- **Cooking in a variety of ways.** If your child doesn't like boiled vegetables then try stir frying, steaming, adding sauce or baking to make the texture different. Often if you don't tell a child what they are eating is a vegetable they won't notice!

- **Add fun dips.** If a child won't eat fruit or vegetables on their own try offering fun dips for them to dunk them in. For example, raw vegetable sticks with hummus or cream cheese, fruit with yogurt, peanut butter, or even a little melted milk chocolate (as a treat) can all make fruit and vegetables much more appetising.

Pocket tip ⚜

Fresh fruit can be frozen to make delicious and healthy ice lollies or frozen yogurt.

GETTING CHILDREN INVOLVED

Another great way to overcome a child's fussiness is to get them actively involved in food preparation and let them help at meal times. Obviously, this depends on the age of the child, and won't work when you are pressed for time; however, most children enjoy helping in the kitchen. Showing them how fun cooking can be is a good way to help them overcome any food dislikes.

Pocket tip ⚘

Letting your child choose what the family eats for dinner once a week (within reason of course!) is also a good way to let them have some control over what they are eating and will mean they are more likely to eat the meal.

Finally, not recommended for every day, but a good way to get children to eat their vegetables is to entice them with good old-fashioned bribery. Offering a yummy dessert or treat at the end of a meal can sometimes be a useful way to get them to clear their plates!

🥕 IF YOUR CHILD WANTS TO 🥕 BECOME VEGETARIAN

If you are a vegetarian then you are likely to be pleased that they want to adopt vegetarianism, but if no one in your family is vegetarian then you may have some concerns. As mentioned earlier in this chapter, the most important thing to remember is that provided a vegetarian diet is well planned and varied then there is no risk to a child's health in becoming a vegetarian.

Try to discuss the reasons why your child wants to become a vegetarian with them calmly and let them explain why they want to stop eating meat. While for some children or teenagers, vegetarianism may be just a phase, for others it can be the start of a lifestyle choice that they will continue throughout their life so make sure you understand their reasons.

DOS AND DON'TS

- **Do** find the time to sit down with your child calmly and listen to their reasons carefully.

- **Do** voice your concerns to your child and discuss ways you can work together to overcome these.

- **Do** research vegetarianism together.

- **Do** make a list together of all vegetarian-friendly foods the family currently eats and try to include more of these foods.

- **Do** explore new vegetarian recipes together.

- **Don't** shout at your child or refuse to let them become a vegetarian.

- **Don't** just continue to give your child the same meal minus the meat: find vegetarian alternatives to ensure their nutritional needs are met.

- **Don't** get stressed – with a little trial and error and some communication you'll soon find a way to make the change of lifestyle work.

Top five things your vegetarian children need to know

1. *It is important to get enough calcium for strong bones and teeth.*
2. *Eating protein is important for energy, growth and development.*
3. *You have to eat vegetables and fruit as a vegetarian – not just vegetarian junk food.*
4. *Iron helps keep you strong and healthy and is good for the blood, so it's important to eat lots of green vegetables.*
5. *Wholegrain foods are high in fibre and great for energy.*

HOW TO HANDLE THE CHANGE

The age of your child or children will affect how much control you have over their diet and how much change you need to handle. Teenagers who are old enough to cook their own meals are less likely to have as much of an impact on family life, although this in itself may be a change as they are taking responsibility for their own diet and wellbeing. However, it is still important to discuss their new diet with them to ensure they are eating a balanced vegetarian diet, as they may not be aware of all their nutritional needs.

If your child is younger and still needs you to cook for them then the practical impact of their new vegetarian diet will be more strongly felt. This does not mean that you or the rest of your family need to become vegetarian – no one should be forced to adopt a diet they are not comfortable with – but it does mean that you may need to become more flexible with your cooking in order to reach a happy compromise. For example, you could cook a vegetarian meal for the whole family three or four times a week and then meals with meat left out, or supplemented with an alternative such as a Quorn product the rest of the time for your vegetarian child.

 ## CHANGES TO BE AWARE OF

WEIGHT AND HEIGHT

Children's growth development and health should be carefully monitored. Most children are weighed and have their height measured at school, but if you are switching to a vegetarian diet it is important that you also keep track to make sure your child is staying healthy. A healthy vegetarian diet is lower in fat so you may need to give your child some high-calorie foods to help boost their calorie intake. Peanut butter, bananas, nuts, milk and cheese are a good way to do this.

BATHROOM VISITS

Vegetarian children may need to visit the bathroom a little more frequently as the vegetarian diet contains more vegetables and fibre. This is not a problem but is something to be aware of.

Pocket tip ⚜

It is worth mentioning to anyone else who cares for your child, such as a teacher or child minder, that they are vegetarian, not only so that they can provide adequate meals but also so that they can keep an eye on your child's health and well-being.

If in doubt, it may be a good idea to consult a dietician or nutritionist who specialises in vegetarian nutrition for children to gain more in-depth advice. Fed well, there is no reason that your child won't thrive and grow on a vegetarian diet.

🥕 GIVING CHILDREN A CHOICE 🥕 IF YOU'RE VEGETARIAN

If you are a vegetarian then it is likely that you will want to bring up your children as vegetarians. Where possible though it is preferable to give children a choice to opt out and eat meat if they want to. If they do decide they want to eat meat then it is important to be supportive and not over-emphasise your disappointment, as a vegetarian diet is not for everyone. One thing that is certain is that children shouldn't be forced to follow your diet as they grow older and gain more independence.

Giving them all of the information and options is vital. While you may not want to cook meat for your children at home if you are a vegetarian, you can buy precooked meat options if they want to continue or start eating meat. It is a good idea to discuss why you don't want to cook meat at home with them, explaining why you don't feel comfortable doing so and perhaps allocate them specific cooking utensils they can use if they are old enough to prepare meat for themselves.

COPING WITH SOCIAL OCCASIONS FOR VEGETARIAN CHILDREN

While eating at home as a vegetarian is easy, sticking to a vegetarian diet outside the home can pose a number of challenges, especially for children. Birthday parties, school lunches and meals at friend's houses can make life difficult for a vegetarian child. With a little forward planning and communication you can make things easier.

It is a good idea to let your child's teacher or school know they are vegetarian as most school canteens now offer a vegetarian option. In schools where a vegetarian option isn't offered then it is a good idea to have a chat to your child's teacher or school head to see if a vegetarian option can be provided, after all it's unlikely your child will be the only vegetarian in the school.

School Regulations 2007

Under the School Regulations 2007 it is not a legal requirement for schools to provide a vegetarian or vegan option for children. However, the regulations do state that the school must assess the dietary needs of its population and prepare suitable meals accordingly. Some children from different cultural or religious backgrounds may not be allowed to eat meat on certain days, or certain kinds of meat at all. The good news is that more and more schools do now offer vegetarian options for children, which non-vegetarian children also enjoy.

Birthday parties, Halloween and Christmas parties can be tricky as many dishes are made using animal products such as jelly, certain sweets, cakes and biscuits. If you want to ensure your child doesn't eat these then it is worth letting the adult in charge know and teaching your child which foods to avoid.

Pocket tip

Try sending their own vegetarian party bag with your child so that the host doesn't feel pressured into providing specialist food.

There is a good range of vegetarian alternatives for popular children's foods so try to offer these to your child (or give them to other parents to dish out at parties) so they don't feel left out.

Contains an animal product	Vegetarian alternative
Jelly contains gelatine	Vegetarian jelly sachets available from most supermarkets and health food stores. Rowntree is usually vegetarian and Marks & Spencer stock vegetarian jelly.
Jelly sweets such as JellyJelly Babies, Fruit Pastilles, Haribo or Wine Gums	Veggie jelly bears. The popular Belly brand is vegetarian and Holland & Barrett stock vegetarian jelly beans.
Meat-flavoured crisps such as prawn crackers	Ready salted, salt and vinegar. Boots clearly labels vegetarian-friendly crisps.

🥕 PACKED LUNCH IDEAS 🥕

No child likes to be different from their friends and you can easily pack a vegetarian packed lunch that won't make them stand out. Here's some ideas:

- vegetarian sandwiches: try hummus and grated carrot, cheese and pickle, Quorn ham and salad

- vegetarian sausage rolls
- vegetarian pasta salad
- homemade fruity flapjack
- homemade banana bread
- chopped fruit in bite-sized pieces
- vegetable crisps
- vegetarian yogurt pot
- carton of juice.

Groups for vegetarian children

- *The Vegetarian Society's Young Veggies group provides advice on being vegetarian, fun recipe ideas and things to get involved with. Visit www.youngveggie.org for more information.*
- *Local vegetarian groups – Veg Soc has a local group finder to find a group in your area at www.vegsoc.org. Most groups welcome older vegetarian children and organise walks, events and campaigning activities.*
- *Most universities have vegetarian and vegan societies that organise fun outings and cooking activities for vegetarians.*
- *Start your own! If you want to introduce your children to other vegetarian children you could think about starting your own group using Facebook or Twitter.*

8

VEGANISM

Veganism is a further extension of vegetarianism in which absolutely no animal products are consumed. This means that not only do vegans avoid meat, dairy and other animal-derived foods but most also avoid wearing animal-sourced clothing or using such products.

Vegans eat a plant-based diet, but this isn't to say that the vegan diet is difficult to follow, particularly for those already familiar with the vegetarian diet. This chapter will explain the philosophy of veganism and illustrate how it differs from vegetarianism, while also providing nutritional information on the vegan diet.

🥕 THE PHILOSOPHY BEHIND VEGANISM 🥕

Much like vegetarianism, there are different motivations behind the vegan lifestyle. Ethical vegans generally promote animal rights as the principal reason to avoid exploiting animal products (see p.9). Environmental vegans lament the energy used and pollutants created in rearing animals for foodstuffs, citing veganism as a partial solution to problems like global warming. Many who choose a vegan lifestyle take a little from both environmentalism and animal rights, whilst focusing on the health benefits of dietary veganism.

Professor Peter Singer of Princeton University, one of the leading proponents of 'ethical veganism', does support what is commonly referred to as 'the Paris Exception'. This permits ethical vegans minor infractions when in a strange place where they are unable to find vegan food – meaning vegetarian alternatives will suffice. For Singer, veganism is not simply an issue of personal purity and therefore such infrequent exceptions do not impugn the ethics of the lifestyle.

HOW IT DIFFERS TO VEGETARIANISM

The vegan diet is similar to the vegetarian diet, with the exception that no animal products whatsoever are consumed. In addition to abstaining from meat, dairy, eggs and animal derivatives such as gelatine are avoided. Many vegans also avoid honey as this is technically an animal product and even wear vegan clothes which have not been made using an animal by-product.

Pocket tip ⚜

Agave nectar is a useful vegan substitute for honey. It is most commonly made in Mexico from blue agave plants, which are similar to aloe vera. It can be bought at most health food shops.

🥕 BENEFITS OF A VEGAN DIET

There are several benefits to eating a vegan diet, including:

- lower blood pressure
- lower body mass index (BMI) and reduced likelihood of obesity
- lower cholesterol levels
- reduced risk of developing degenerative diseases such as cancer, heart conditions, diabetes, etc
- longer life expectancy.

Pocket fact 🌶

According to the Vegan Society, vegans in developed countries are two BMI points less than their meat-eating counterparts. In other words, they're slimmer, less at risk of diabetes and tend to have lower blood pressure!

Body Mass Index (BMI)

The BMI scale takes a person's weight (in kg) and divides it by the square root of their height (in metres) to give them a score which indicates their body size. The sliding scale is used by medical professionals to objectively discuss weight issues with patients and many people use their BMI score to monitor their own health. The 'normal' range is 18.5–25, with a score of below 16.0 being 'severely underweight' and over 30 being 'obese'. BMI is intended to measure an average person taking on average nutrition, so is not an absolute rule (as it may not accurately reflect someone who is extremely tall or short).

COMMON MYTHS ABOUT VEGANISM

Here are a few myths surrounding veganism.

MYTH: THE VEGAN DIET IS LACKING IN PROTEIN

Many people incorrectly assume that because vegans don't eat meat, dairy or eggs their diets must be lacking in protein. In fact, vegans can easily get enough protein from dark green leafy vegetables, nuts, seeds, legumes, grains, tofu and soya.

MYTH: VEGANS ONLY EAT FRUIT AND VEGETABLES

Yes, vegans do eat fruit and vegetables but it is certainly not the case that this is all they eat. A healthy and wholesome vegan diet is also packed full with beans, pulses, wholegrains, nuts, seeds, soya products and tofu.

MYTH: VEGANISM IS UNHEALTHY AND DANGEROUS

A balanced vegan diet could not be further from unhealthy or dangerous if it tried. Packed full of nutritious fruit, vegetables, pulses, nuts and wholegrains, etc it is vitamin- and mineral-rich and low in fat.

Veganism, similarly to other diets, is only regarded as dangerous if it is not nutritionally balanced and if it avoids fresh produce.

Pocket tip ⚜

Eating large quantities of vegetables, fruit and low-fat protein foods, such as lentils, beans and wholegrains can improve diges-tion, as they are less acidic than animal products and easier for the body to digest. Try to eat as wide a variety of fresh foods as possible for optimum health.

🥕 DIETARY REQUIREMENTS 🥕 FOR VEGANS

Vegans have to work a little harder than vegetarians to ensure that their daily intake of vitamins and minerals is met. While it certainly isn't that hard to do, for those new to veganism it may seem a bit daunting. As with the vegetarian diet it is important that you incorporate as wide a range of fruits, vegetables, pulses, and wholegrains into your diet as possible to ensure that you are not lacking in these.

The five nutrients that vegans may lack if a healthy diet isn't followed are:

- vitamin D
- vitamin B12
- iron
- selenium
- omega-3 fatty acids.

However, it's easy to get enough of these in a vegan diet provided you eat the right foods, examples of which are included below.

Pocket tip 🌾

Red, orange and yellow peppers, carrots and sweetcorn are a good source of carotenoids, which are powerful antioxidants that help protect against cancer.

ESSENTIAL NUTRIENTS

It is important that vegans ensure their diets contain the RDAs of the essential nutrients to help maintain a fit and healthy body. Refer back to Chapter 2 (p.27) for more nutritional information but the following sections give some tips on which foods to include in a vegan diet to ensure you're getting all of the nutrients you need.

Vitamin A (retinol)

Vegans can get vitamin A from these foods:

- green leafy vegetables
- carrots
- soya products
- tomatoes
- grapefruit
- pecan nuts.

Pocket fact 🥕

Remember the saying that carrots help you see in the dark? Well it's true and vegans will find a good source of vitamin A in the beta-carotene in carrots, which is more easily absorbed if the carrot is cooked or juiced. Blitz two carrots, an apple, and a tablespoon of fresh grated ginger in a blender for a healthy smoothie.

Vitamin B1 (thiamine)

Vegan foods are rich in this vitamin, so here is just a short list:

- dark green leafy vegetables such as broccoli, curly kale and spinach
- fruit
- wholegrains
- peanuts – try to avoid heavily salted or roasted and stick to plain.

Pocket tip ✤

Alcohol and coffee can destroy the benefits of vitamin B1, so try to avoid drinking too much of either and stick to soft drinks or herbal teas instead.

Vitamin B2 (riboflavin)

Good sources of vitamin B2 for vegans include:

- brown rice
- green leafy vegetables
- mushrooms
- fortified breakfast cereals
- yeast or a yeast extract product such as Marmite.

Vitamin B12

Good sources of B12 for vegans include:

- fortified soya products
- fortified yeast extract such as Marmite or similar
- fortified breakfast cereals
- quality B12 food supplements.

Vitamin C (ascorbic acid)

The good news is vegans are likely to have plenty of vitamin C in their diets as it is found in a wide variety of fruits and vegetables. Good sources include:

- citrus fruits, in particular kiwis and oranges

- green vegetables

- peppers

- sweet potatoes

- fruit juices

- berries

- tomatoes.

Pocket fact 🌶

Sweet potatoes are much more nutritious than white potatoes and are a slow-release food, meaning you stay fuller for longer. Try baking them and stuffing with mixed beans for a healthy and easy vegan meal. Remember that beans are one of your five a day!

Vitamin D

Vegans are more likely than vegetarians to be lacking in this vitamin as many of the essential amino acids found in dairy produce help the body absorb vitamin D. Vegans should ensure they get plenty of substitutes rich in vitamin D. For more information about vitamin D deficiency, see Chapter 2, p.30.

For vegans the best source of vitamin D comes from:

- soya alternatives such as milk and yogurt

- fortified breakfast cereals

- mushrooms

- fortified fruit juices
- sunlight.

> *Pocket tip* ⚜
> *While being careful to avoid sunburn, try to expose your skin to sunlight for around 15 minutes a day as this will help boost your vitamin D levels.*

Vitamin E

Vegans are likely to eat plenty of vitamin E as it is found in the following vegan favourites:

- nuts and seeds
- soya beans
- green vegetables
- wholegrains
- wheat germ – often found in breakfast cereals.

Folic acid

It is a good idea for all pregnant women, including vegans, to make sure they are getting enough folic acid. Good sources include:

- green leafy vegetables, in particular broccoli and curly kale
- peas
- asparagus
- chickpeas
- brown rice
- wholewheat bread
- yeast or yeast extract spread.

Iron

This mineral is good for the blood and muscles, and vegans can get their daily dose of iron from the following foods:

- green leafy vegetables such as spinach, watercress, curly kale and broccoli
- dried fruits such as apricots and figs
- fortified breakfast cereals – try to opt for less sugary cereals
- wholemeal bread
- pulses.

Calcium

Calcium can be found in the following vegan foods:

- nuts and seeds
- leafy green vegetables
- pulses and legumes such as kidney beans and lentils
- wholegrains
- tofu
- orange juice.

For vegans, soya alternatives or nut milk can still provide a good source of calcium when accompanied with other foods from the above list. Vegans should aim to get at least 500mg of calcium each day by eating calcium-rich foods or by taking a supplement.

Potassium

Good sources of potassium for vegans include:

- bananas
- avocados
- dried or fresh apricots
- potatoes – white and sweet

- raisins
- pumpkin.

Pocket tip ⚜

Salt (sodium) has the opposite effect to potassium, as it increases the amount of potassium and calcium the body loses, so it is a good idea to reduce your sodium intake and eat plenty of fruit and vegetables. Other seasonings such as herbs and spices can be used as a healthy flavour replacement.

Magnesium

Vegan foods that are high in magnesium include:

- green leafy vegetables
- wholegrains
- raisins
- pulses
- brazil nuts
- artichokes.

Pocket tip ⚜

Try adding marinated roasted artichokes to pasta or salad dishes for a tasty magnesium-rich meal.

Zinc

Some zinc-rich vegan foods are:

- brown rice
- wholegrains
- fortified cereals

- pumpkin seeds
- beans
- potatoes.

Selenium

Vegans need to ensure they get enough selenium as it helps keep the immune system strong and is good for liver function. Good sources of selenium include:

- brazil nuts
- eggs
- wholewheat bread
- watercress
- cheese
- sunflower seeds
- peas
- mangos.

Pocket tip ✤

According to the Vegan Society, a 30g handful of nuts each day may help to increase life expectancy by two years. You might want to keep a pack of nuts in your bag or desk to snack on, but remember that nuts are high in fat so try not to eat a whole bag in one go.

Carbohydrates

Sources of good carbohydrates for vegans include:

- wholewheat pasta
- brown rice – other varieties are also fine
- noodles

- wholegrain or granary bread

- potatoes

- fruit – especially bananas, mangos or pineapples

- vegetables – especially potatoes, carrots or beets.

Protein

Good vegan sources of protein include:

- nuts and seeds

- beans, pulses and legumes

- soya products

- tofu

- peanut butter

- quinoa

- mushrooms.

Pocket tip ⚜

Wholegrains are higher in protein than fruit, which contain more vitamins and minerals. Try eating a good range of both to boost your nutrient intake.

Essential fatty acids, omega-3 and omega-6

Vegans need to make sure they get plenty of omega-3 and omega-6, known as essential fatty acids, in their diets in order to maintain a healthy heart and reduce the risk of heart-related disease. Omega-3 and omega-6 are commonly found in oily fish and eggs, but there are plenty of vegan alternatives that contain high doses. See Chapter 2 for more information.

Pocket tip ❧

Eating a breakfast packed full of ground flaxseeds and nuts is a good way to get your daily omega-3 fatty essential acid intake. The hard shells of the flaxseed prevent the nutrients from being absorbed, so try grinding them first or adding to a smoothie and blending well.

FAMOUS VEGANS

Veganism has gained popularity among many well-known figures who have chosen to eat a vegan diet because of ethical and health reasons.

BILL AND CHELSEA CLINTON

Chelsea Clinton, the daughter of former US president Bill Clinton, has followed a vegan diet for a number of years and even served a vegan wedding breakfast for her guests at her wedding. In 2010, Bill himself adopted the diet to help lose weight and return to good health following heart problems. He has accredited the plant-based diet for helping him return to the weight he was at high school and for improving his health.

Pocket fact ✐

Bill Clinton is not a strict vegan as he very occasionally eats fish; however, many vegan groups still argue that he has helped bring veganism to the masses by making it appear manageable.

ALICIA SILVERSTONE

A passionate vegan, the actress Alicia Silverstone has written a book called *The Kind Diet* about veganism, in which she shares how and why she became a vegan, the way it changed her life for the better and how readers can do the same.

MOBY

Moby has been a vegan for over 24 years and has written a number of essays that highlight his concerns for the environment and for animals. In the inside jacket of his 1996 album *Animal Rights*, Moby sums up his stance on animal protection simply by stating, 'If you don't want to be beaten, imprisoned, mutilated, killed, or tortured, then you shouldn't condone such behaviour toward anyone, be they human or not'.

SCOTT JUREK

The accomplished ultra marathon runner Scott Jurek easily clocks up around 140 miles a week in running and has competed in some of the most gruelling endurance races in the world, such as the notorious Badwater Ultramarathon, a 135-mile race that begins in Death Valley and ends halfway up Mount Whitney, which he won while eating a 100% vegan diet.

Jurek apparently grew up eating a traditional diet of meat and potatoes but gradually began to cut meat and fish out of his diet at college, before dropping the dairy to become a fully-fledged vegan. As an ultra marathon runner, obviously Jurek's energy and calorie requirements differ from the average person's, but he claims he gets all the fuel his body needs from a nutritious vegan diet.

Pocket fact

Before setting off on a long run (seven hours plus!) Jurek drinks a mega 1,000-calorie smoothie made of oil, almonds, bananas, blueberries, salt, vanilla, dried coconut, a few dates and brown rice protein powder.

CARL LEWIS

Track and field athlete Carl Lewis has attributed his success in athletics to his vegan diet, saying that his best year of track competition was the first year he ate a vegan diet.

Pocket fact

Health experts say that one of the reasons the vegan diet is so useful for athletes and sportspeople is because it meets all their protein, complex carbohydrate and nutritional requirements without containing the saturated fat levels of meat.

VEGAN COOKING

The main thing that differentiates vegan from vegetarian cooking is that none of the goods used are animal sourced. Nevertheless, vegan cooking can be varied and healthy, and doesn't mean that you have to sacrifice taste in order to make a dish vegan.

VEGAN FOOD REPLACEMENTS

Some of the food replacements vegans can eat and use in cooking are:

Vegetarian option	Vegan replacement
Dairy milk	Soya, nut, hemp, oat or rice milk
	Try 'So good' or Provamel Soya milk
Dairy cheese and yogurt	Vegan cheese and soya yogurt
	Try Cheezly, Sheese and Alpro Yoghurt
Scrambled eggs	Scrambled tofu
	Try the Cauldron Tofu range
Double cream	Soya cream
	Try Alpro Soya cream
Butter	Vegetable oil
	Try 'Pure' margarine
Honey	Agave nectar
	Visit a health food store to find this

VEGAN CHEESE

Many people decide to become a vegan after following a vegetarian diet for a number of years and see it as the last step in achieving their ethical or environmental goal. At this stage, non-dairy milks and yogurts are usually easy to replace, but cheese is often the last animal product that a vegan gives up as vegan cheeses don't taste exactly like the real thing.

Pocket fact 🖎

Vegan cheese is made from soya and vegetable oil to form either hard or soft cheeses. It can be eaten raw in salads and sandwiches or used in cooking.

The following products can be useful and interesting alternatives to cheese.

- **Sheese vegan cheese: strong cheddar style.** An original vegan cheddar cheese recipe made using vegetable oil, oat fibre and dairy-free lactic acid among other ingredients. Good for sandwiches, grilling on toast or eating on crackers.

- **Parmazano dairy-free cheese**. A vegan alternative to parmesan, predominately made using soya flour and palm oil. Good grated into pasta dishes, on jacket potatoes or in risottos where the taste of cheese is desired. Some supermarkets may stock vegan cheeses, otherwise health food stores are a good option. Alternatively, try www.goodnessdirect.co.uk or www.redwoodfoods.co.uk.

- **Free and easy dairy-free cheese sauce.** Sold as a dried powder and made using rice flour, cornstarch, vegetable oil, dried cereals and vegetables among other ingredients. The powder can be mixed with water or soya milk to make a creamy cheese sauce for dishes such as lasagne, pasta bake or cauliflower cheese.

Make your own vegan cheese

It is surprisingly easy to make your own homemade vegan cheese. Here is a simple recipe to make a soft and spreadable vegan cheese.

Ingredients
- *1 cup of soya flour*
- *1 tsp yeast extract*
- *1 tsp dried basil*
- *Pinch salt and pepper*
- *1 small tub of soft vegan margarine*

Method
1. *Melt the margarine, and mix in the flour, yeast, herbs and salt and pepper.*
2. *Pour into the empty margarine tub and refrigerate until set.*

Fresh herbs or nuts can be added as an alternative.

VEGAN BREAD

Many of the big brands in the UK produce bread that is perfectly acceptable for vegans. After all, most bread is simply flour, water, yeast and salt. Always check before buying, though. Here's a list of some which are confirmed as being suitable.

- **Kingsmill.** Medium White, Toastie White, Soft White Farmhouse, Danish White, Seeded Batch, Wholemeal Medium, Stoneground Wholemeal Batch, Stoneground Wholemeal Batch Crusty, All in One Medium Healthy Inside.

- **Hovis.** Soft white, Best of both, Wholemeal, White farmhouse, Wholemeal farmhouse, Original granary, Wholemeal granary, Original wheatgerm, Seed sensations light and nutty, Seed sensations rich and roasted.

Make your own bread

As some supermarket brands are not exactly the healthiest or cheapest option, it can be a good idea to make your own bread. The easiest way to do this is with a bread machine, though it is certainly possible without.

Vegetable Bread

Ingredients
- 225ml tomato juice
- 225ml water
- 1 (7g) sachet fast action bread yeast
- 5 tbsp agave nectar
- 4 tbsp olive oil
- 1/2 bunch fresh parsley, chopped
- 3 spring onions, chopped
- 2 cloves garlic
- 1 carrot, grated
- 1 courgette, grated
- 1 tsp salt
- 800g bread flour

Method
1. Gently heat the tomato juice and water in a saucepan until warm to the touch. Pour into a large warmed bowl, and then add the yeast and the agave nectar, stirring to dissolve the yeast. Allow the mixture to rest until the yeast is creamy.
2. Mix in the oil, parsley, onion, garlic, carrot, courgette and salt. Add 1/4 of the flour, and stir until smooth. Gradually add more flour, a little at a time, until a firm dough is formed.
3. Knead the dough for 5 minutes on a lightly floured surface.

4. *Place dough in an oiled bowl, and turn to coat the surface completely. Allow to rise in a warm place until doubled in size.*

5. *Push down the dough and divide it into halves. Form two loaves, and put into greased 23x12cm (9x5 inch) loaf tins. Allow to rise for another 45 minutes, or until loaves have doubled in size.*

6. *Bake at 220°C / Gas mark 6 for about 30 minutes, until golden brown.*

Remove from tins and allow to cool on a wire rack.

RECIPE IDEAS

SCRAMBLED TOFU WITH ONIONS AND MUSHROOMS ON TOASTED RYE BREAD

Serves 2

Ingredients

- 1 block of tofu drained and dried

- ½ tsp turmeric (this will give the tofu an attractive flavour and colour)

- 1tbsp of olive oil

- 1 large white onion, finely sliced

- 1 clove garlic, finely sliced

- 8 button mushrooms, roughly chopped

- Salt and pepper

- Fresh parsley

Method

1. Scramble up the tofu in a bowl using a fork and mix in the turmeric and set aside.

2. Fry the onions and garlic in the olive oil in a large non-stick pan until a golden brown.

3. Add the tofu, mushrooms and parsley, and season. Cook over a medium heat for 10 minutes or until the tofu starts to brown.

4. Serve immediately on top of slices of toasted rye bread.

FRUIT AND OAT SMOOTHIE

Serves 1

Ingredients

- 1 banana
- 1 kiwi
- 5 strawberries
- Handful of blueberries
- 1tbsp of porridge oats or wheat germ
- 1tbsp of omega seed mix
- Quarter of a pint of soya milk

Method

1. Roughly chop all the fruit and blend in a food blender.

2. Add the oats and seeds and continue to blend.

3. Gradually add the milk and blitz until smooth. A couple of ice cubes can be added here to make the drink cool, or it can be placed in the fridge for a couple of minutes.

VEGAN PITTA BREADS FILLED WITH HUMMUS AND BALSAMIC ROASTED VEGETABLES

Serves 2

Ingredients

- 1 large red onion, roughly chopped
- 10 cherry tomatoes

- 1 red pepper, sliced roughly
- 1 yellow pepper, sliced roughly
- 3 cloves garlic, whole
- 1 courgette, sliced
- ½ aubergine, sliced
- Handful of fresh basil leaves
- 2tbsp balsamic vinegar and olive oil mixed
- Pinch each of salt and pepper

Method

1. Heat the oven to 180°C and place all the vegetables in a large roasting tin.

2. Drizzle with the balsamic dressing and roast for 20 minutes or until cooked.

3. Allow to cool.

4. Spread hummus in the pitta and fill with the vegetables. Serve immediately.

TOMATO AND BASIL SOUP

Serves 3/4

Ingredients

- 2 large punnets of tomatoes – around 16 tomatoes, roughly chopped
- 1 large red onion, sliced
- 3 cloves of garlic
- 1tbsp olive oil
- Bunch of fresh basil
- Salt and pepper
- Vegan cream

Method

1. Heat the oven to 180°C. Place the tomatoes, onion and garlic on the baking tray and drizzle with olive oil. Season and roast for 15–20 minutes.

2. In a blender, blend the roasted tomatoes, garlic and onion and add the fresh basil, roughly torn.

3. Pour into a large saucepan and heat over a medium heat. Add a dollop of the cream to give the soup a rich creamy flavour. Serve immediately with fresh bread.

Pocket tip ❧

If you enjoy baking bread, try replacing 10% of the flour with ground flaxseed to obtain a good source of omega-3 fats.

VEGETABLE THAI GREEN CURRY WITH COCONUT MILK, VEGETABLES AND TOFU

Serves 2

Ingredients

- 1tbsp rapeseed oil
- 1 block of firm tofu, diced and dried
- 1 small aubergine, diced
- 1 red pepper, roughly sliced
- 1 pack of baby sweetcorn
- 1 pack of mangetout
- 1 can of coconut milk
- 200g (dry weight) Thai sticky rice

For the Thai curry paste:

- 1 stalk of lemongrass

- 3 green chilli, deseeded and sliced
- 1 shallot finely sliced
- 5 cloves of garlic, finely sliced
- 1 inch galangal (Thai ginger), finely sliced
- Handful of fresh coriander
- Handful of fresh basil
- 1tsp cumin
- 1tsp white pepper
- 1tsp ground coriander
- 3tbsp soy sauce
- Juice of 1 lime
- 1tsp of brown sugar

Method

1. To make the Thai curry paste, mash all the ingredients together in a pestle and mortar or blitz in a food processor.

2. In a large non-stick frying pan heat the oil and add the paste, heating until fragrant. Then fry the tofu for 5 minutes before adding the vegetables. Stir fry for a further 3 minutes. Reduce the heat and pour in the coconut milk and allow to simmer for 30 minutes.

Serve immediately in small bowls with the sticky Thai rice.

Pocket tip ⚜

To make the perfect Thai rice shape press a portion of rice into a small bowl, place a plate over the bowl and turn over. You should now have a neat mould of rice to accompany your curry.

THREE BEAN CHILLI WITH BROWN RICE, GUACAMOLE AND SALSA

Serves 4

Ingredients

- 1 red chilli, sliced
- 2 cloves garlic
- 1 large red onion, chopped
- 1 red pepper, chopped
- 1 yellow pepper, chopped
- 2 cans of mixed beans
- 1 can of kidney beans
- 1 can of chopped tomatoes
- 1tbsp tomato puree
- 1 can of sweetcorn
- 1tsp of cumin
- 1tsp chilli powder
- 1tsp dried coriander

Method

1. Fry the onions, garlic and chilli in 2 tsp of oil in a large non-stick pan. Add the peppers and cook for a further 5 minutes.

2. Add the beans, tomatoes, tomato puree and seasonings and stir well. Reduce the heat and stir occasionally, cooking for 30 minutes. If the chilli starts to stick or seems too dry add a little water.

3. Serve immediately with brown rice, green salad, guacamole, salsa, and a small handful of vegan nachos.

Alternative suggestion

Use vegetarian or vegan mince as an alternative to mixed beans.

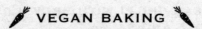 VEGAN BAKING

Traditionally, most cakes, breads and biscuits are not suitable for vegans as they contain egg and/or dairy but the good news is that there are other ingredients that can be used to rustle up a range of delicious and tempting vegan cakes, breads, cookies and so on.

There are a number of egg replacements vegans can use in cooking:

- chick pea or soya flour mixed with a drop of water
- arrowroot, soya flour and water
- vegan egg replacement powder mixed with water
- blended tofu
- mashed bananas
- vegetable oil
- soya, coconut or nut milk.

Great websites for vegan recipes
- *The Vegan Table:* www.vegantable.com
- *Post Punk Kitchen:* www.theppk.com
- *Vegan Village:* www.veganvillage.co.uk

Pocket tip ⚜

Bananas work as a good replacement in sweet dishes such as cakes and puddings but not in savoury dishes. Try a dried vegan egg replacement instead or vegetable oil.

VEGAN SNACKS AND TREATS

As a healthy snack choose from the following:

- piece of fruit such as apple, banana, orange, etc

- carrot sticks with hummus dip

- oat cakes topped with peanut butter

- handful of vegetable crisps.

For the occasional treat, try the vegan chocolate, sweets, biscuits and cakes which are readily available at health food shops, most supermarkets and online.

Pocket tip ❧

Celebrate World Vegan Day (WVD) on 1 November by taking part in a vegan event. Started in 1994 to celebrate the founding of the vegan movement by Donald Watson, WVD consists of food fares, campaigns and cooking demonstrations. Visit www.worldveganday.org.uk for more information.

VEGAN SHOPPING

A variety of websites have been mentioned already, although there really is a wealth of different places to buy vegan products across the UK.

- **Bourgeois Boheme** is a shop in Notting Hill which is run by vegans and stocks fashionable shoes for men and women. They also have a website from which you can order online www.bboheme.com.

- **Feel Good Handbags** (www.feelgoodhandbags.com) is an online store which has a wide range of handbags which are cruelty-free and vegan-friendly.

- **Etsy** is an online network with a variety of independent sellers and craftsmen pursuing a vegan lifestyle and creating vegan products. There are many different items for sale, just search for 'vegan' to find all sorts of clothes. Go to www.etsy.com.

- **Superdrug** has a full range of vegan cosmetics called 'Simply Pure'. The range includes a light moisturiser, face cream, cleansing face mask, toner and eye make-up remover. They are all BUAV accredited, suitable for sensitive skin and also affordable!

- **Vegan Cake Direct** has a variety of cakes for all occasions, from Victoria sponges to carrot cakes and fruit buns. Visit www.vegancakedirect.co.uk.

- **Vegan Store** is a great resource which not only stocks many types of vegan foods, but also shoes and household products (cleaning, cosmetics, etc.). The site itself is run by vegans and is easy to search through. Go to www.veganstore.co.uk.

- **Cupcake Britain** (www.cupcakebritain.co.uk) produce a delicious range of cupcakes which you can order online. They combine veganism with temptingly delicious baking!

- **The Vegan Village** (www.veganvillage.co.uk) provides an extensive directory of vegan and vegetarian stores from across the country selling everything from vegan gummy sweets to high-class vegan fashion accessories.

VEGAN RESTAURANTS

Squeek Restaurant

Located in Nottingham, Squeek is a fantastic veggie restaurant with loads of vegan dishes. A monthly change to the menu makes recommendations difficult, but you'll definitely see beautifully presented meals which tempt even meat-eaters with their veggie wiles (www.vegan-nottingham.co.uk).

Demuths Restaurant

Demuths in Bath is an up-market and inspiring restaurant which puts out delicious vegetarian and vegan dishes to suit any palate, as demonstrated with the slew of awards it has won over the last few years (www.demuths.co.uk).

222 Veggie Vegan

This restaurant in West Kensington offers a wide selection of light bites and full meals, catering for both eating in and take-away. Their vegan chefs are imaginative and talented so you'll be in for a treat. Their millet rissoles are a particular favourite (www.222veggivegan.com).

The Spirited Palace

The Spirited Palace in Crystal Palace is a Caribbean inspired restaurant which puts out both vegan cuisine and raw vegan food. Their spicy delights are well worth sampling and their soya milkshakes come highly recommended (www.thespiritedpalace.com).

The 13th Note

The 13th Note is a music venue, bar and veggie/vegan cafe in Glasgow. Their menu is mainly vegan, with tempting salads and some specialities like their take on haggis. It's well worth dropping in for a concert, a drink and a vegan meal (www.13thnote.co.uk).

Itadaki Zen

This is a Japanese restaurant in Kings Cross which eschews tradition to produce delicious Asian vegan food. This is a popular eatery which has been frequently praised for its healthy approach to cooking (www.itadakizen.com).

Manna

Manna is perhaps the premier vegan restaurant in London. Located in Primrose Hill, their daily menu is based on what's in season and what's delicious at that precise moment (www.mannav.com).

Rainbow Cafe

This is Cambridge's only dedicated vegetarian restaurant and has a good range of vegan-friendly dishes. They produce a fusion of dishes with worldwide inspiration, from enchiladas to Jamaican vegetarian patties (www.rainbowcafe.co.uk).

Vbites

Vbites in Brighton is a modern vegan restaurant with a good variety of options. From meat alternatives like vegan burgers to vegan pizza and pasta, this is a delicious option when visiting the shore (www.vbites.com).

Heavenly

Heavenly is a recently opened Glasgow vegan venue which has tempting pastas, burgers and even kebabs. They specialise in food, drink and music, making it a fantastic place to spend some time (www.heavenlyglasgow.co.uk).

The Vegan Society

Founded in 1944, The Vegan Society (www.vegansociety.com) offers support and guidance for those interested in becoming a vegan or for those already following a vegan diet.

This is a useful resource for both vegans and vegetarians for finding information on nutrition and lifestyle, new recipes to try and to search for places to eat out in the UK and Ireland. The website also includes a selection of interesting video clips on the vegan diet and lifestyle such as: being pregnant and vegan or being an athlete and vegan.
